Training Games
for
Managing Change

Training Games
for
Managing Change

50 Activities for Trainers and Consultants

Suzanne Adele Schmidt, Ph.D.

Joanne G. Sujansky, Ph.D.

McGraw-Hill

New York   San Francisco   Washington, D.C.   Auckland   Bogotá
Caracas   Lisbon   London   Madrid   Mexico City   Milan
Montreal   New Delhi   San Juan   Singapore
Sydney   Tokyo   Toronto

McGraw-Hill

A Division of The McGraw·Hill Companies

2 3 4 5 6 7 8 9 0   BKM / BKM   9 0 9 8 7 6 5 4 3 2 1 0 9

ISBN 0-07-134308-3

The sponsoring editor for this book was Richard Narramore, the editing supervisor was Fred Dahl, the editing liaison was Patricia V. Amoroso, and the production supervisor was Modestine Cameron. It was typeset in New Baskerville by Inkwell Publishing Services.

Printed and bound by Book-mart Press, Inc.

McGraw-Hill Books are available at special quantity discounts to use as premiums and sales promotions, or for use in corporate training programs. For more information, please write to the Director of Special Sales, McGraw-Hill, 11 West 19th Street, New York, NY 10011. Or contact your local bookstore.

I dedicate this book to:

My parents, Alice and Richard Schmidt, Sr., with gratitude for their lessons about accepting change courageously and playing wholeheartedly.

My best friend, Dan Davis, with great thanks to him for being my changemate and playmate.

SUZANNE ADELE SCHMIDT, PH.D.

I dedicate this book to:

My husband, Chuck Sujansky, and our children, Cara, Justin, and Jenna, for their love, encouragement, and support.

My parents, Mary Ellen and John Genova, for their love and guidance.

JOANNE G. SUJANSKY, PH.D.

Contents

KEY: *N=none; S=some; M=moderate

Contents

	Page Number	Inevitability of Change	Understanding Reactions to Change	Taking Personal Responsibility for Change	Skills Needed for Creating and Implementing Change	Resources for Creating and Implementing Change	Leading Others Through Change	Uses Art, Music, or Literature	Includes Physical Activity*	Play Time (minutes)
Content-Driven Activities	83									
13. A Trip Down Memory Change Lane	85	•							S	30
14. We've Looked at Change…	87				•	•	•		N	30
15. Musical Chairs	89	•	•				•	•	M	30
16. Concentration	93		•					•	N	20
17. Charades	99		•	•					M	60
18. Twenty Questions	117				•		•		N	30
19. Dive Right In!	161		•				•		N	20
20. Change Muscle Builder	163				•	•			N	30
21. My Hero! My Heroine!	167				•				N	25
22. You're in Control	171			•					N	20
23. Ready … Aim!	175			•	•				N	20
24. Hot Buttons	179				•		•		N	30
25. Change Debate	185		•						N	30
26. Back to the Future	187						•	•	N	45
27. Raindrops on Roses	191					•	•		N	30
28. Obstacle Illusion	197					•		•	S	45
29. Wrestling Resistance	199						•		N	30
30. *These* Are the Good Old Days!	203	•							N	25

KEY: *N=none; S=some; M=moderate

Contents

KEY: *N=none; S=some; M=moderate

Acknowledgments

Writing a book "in our spare time" demanded that we juggle many balls of various sizes, shapes, and weights at one time. Fortunately, we had people helping us keep these balls in the air throughout the long, arduous process of completing and revising the manuscript. We gratefully acknowledge our fellow jugglers.

C—Clients and Colleagues

We have been blessed over the years with clients and colleagues who have been willing to "play for change." Their enthusiasm, encouragement, and feedback have proven invaluable, and we are deeply grateful to each one.

H—Heroes and Heroines

We were cared for by an inner circle of family and friends who fed and nurtured us, and who made sure that the mundane responsibilities of life were handled when we were unable to muster the energy. Thanks!

A—Artist

During our more creative moments, we visualized beautiful artwork that we unfortunately did not have the talent to produce. Then along came twelve-year-old Derek Reed to bring our visions to life. Watch for him to be featured at an art show in the future.

N—Nemocolin Woodlands Resort & Spa

We committed ourselves to writing this book while sitting poolside and sipping tropical beverages. This western Pennsylvania year round resort provided us with refuge, renewal, and a place to write at numerous points along the way. We highly recommend it.

G—Game Aficionados

While exploring the idea for the book, we tapped into the expertise of a loyal band of game lovers (aka our focus group), who were there for the kickoff, were there with feedback, and who will be there for our publication celebration. We couldn't have done it without you.

E—Editorial Assistants

As two creative, right-brained individuals, not so fond of details, we might have struggled more with the book than we actually did. We give thanks for the expert assistance of Sharon Umberger, whose eagle eyes and word processing skills gave us a flawless manuscript, and we extend our gratitude to Jennifer Kissel and Rae Thompson for their keen editorial and writing assistance. Their work greatly enhanced the book.

Facilitating Organizational Change through Training

Introduction

Going through organizational change is, in many ways, like going through an amusement park funhouse. While organizational change is a lot more serious, the range of ways in which people approach and react to such change is similar to the range of ways people react to funhouse surprises. Some people approach the experience cautiously, with great concentration. Some people run through it light-heartedly, impatient to see what's next. Still others refuse to enter, choosing instead to find something more calm and reassuring.

Knowing what to expect can make organizational change somewhat easier, while having someone to guide you through the experience can make it easier still. *Training Games for Managing Change* is designed to help you, the training facilitator, prepare organization leaders, managers, and employees to face the surprises of organizational change.

Facilitator's Role in Change Management

It is the facilitator's role in change management to provide training that addresses the needs of people who react differently to change. The facilitator must bring together people who love the process of change, with its malleable forms and unpredictable twists and turns, and those who are terrified of the unknown. Whether an employee of the organization going through change or an outside contractor, the facilitator helps all organization members gain perspective on change and their reactions to it. An effective facilitator helps people keep pace with organizational changes and perhaps even learn to enjoy the process of change itself.

Planning for Change Management Training

Change abounds in today's organizations. The business news regularly features stories of downsizing, right-sizing, reorganizations, mergers, acquisitions, manufacturing plant relocations, and buyouts. Managers and employees are being asked to do more with less, implement new systems, meet the demands of a global marketplace, and even take pay or benefit reductions. Change management training facilitators can encourage organizational leaders to recognize and address the loss and confusion that accompanies such changes. They can help all members of an organization undergoing change to understand their own and others' attitudes about change.

The best time to teach change management skills is when your organization first publicly announces major changes. As you plan your change management training, be sure to keep the following considerations and questions in mind:

1. Content Considerations
   - What is the focus of the training?
   - How far into the change process is the organization?
   - What is your audience's experience with organizational change?
   - Do your audience members have management responsibilities?

2. Design Consideration
   - Will you be training teams?
   - What are your defined training objectives?
   - How will you reinforce content?

3. Marketing Considerations
   - How will you get senior management to sponsor change management training?

Content Considerations

The purpose of your organization's change management training may differ based on 1) the stage of change in which an organization finds itself; 2) your training audience's experience with organizational change; and 3) whether or not the participants have management responsibilities. Change management training can focus on any one or more of the following content areas:

- The inevitability of change
- Understanding reactions to change
- Taking personal responsibility for change
- Coping skills required for creating and implementing change
- Resources needed for creating and implementing change
- Leading others through change

A discussion of each content area follows. In addition, the matrix located in the table of contents identifies the content areas addressed by each of the 50 activities.

The Inevitability of Change

When people first hear of an impending organizational change, they often express shock. After the shock dissipates, they usually realize that change is a natural part of life. Change management training provides participants with a forum for recognizing the inevitability of change. This aspect of change management training can be especially helpful when an organizational change is first introduced. It can also be applied to organizations and individuals experiencing non-stop change. Examples of activities found in this book that address this aspect of change include You Oughta' Be in Pictures and A Trip Down Memory Lane.

Understanding Reactions to Change

Different people respond differently to change, in part influenced by how much change they have experienced. Hearing similar viewpoints assures participants that they are not alone in their reactions, while hearing different viewpoints sensitizes participants and broadens their perspectives. Examples of activities that address reactions to change include It's in the Cards and I'd Like to Get to Know You.

Taking Personal Responsibility for Change

Many employees have experienced some level of organizational change, but not all have been successful at coping with it. Employees who understand and responsibly handle their part in organizational change are more successful at implementing it. Change management training can help individuals recognize their personal responsibility and the importance of staying actively involved in the change process. Activities such as A Journey into the Future and You're in Control provide participants opportunities to reflect on how they personally can shape the outcome of current changes.

Skills Needed for Creating and Implementing Change

Schools do not teach change management skills. Consequently people often stumble through change without knowing what skills could help them. Change management training gives employees the chance to identify the skills necessary for creating and implementing change. Two activities that highlight essential skills are Change Muscle Builder and My Hero! My Heroine!

Resources Needed for Creating and Implementing Change

When facing change, people often believe that they must carry the burden of dealing with change without the help of other people, other services, or other tools. They need to be reminded about the resources available to them, especially if they are less experienced with organizational change. Packing a New Bag and Obstacle Illusion both address this aspect of change.

Leading Others through Change

Employees need to be guided through change by their managers, who may be ill-prepared for the task and experiencing a wide range of emotions themselves.

Change management training offers a vehicle for managers to deal with their own reactions and become more aware of their employees' reactions. Back to the Future and Wrestling Resistance both offer opportunities for insights into individual responses to change.

Design Considerations

As you design a change management training program for your organization, it is important to determine whether you will be working with teams, identify your training objectives, and utilize varied instructional methodologies. Each of these considerations is discussed here.

Working with Teams

Your training audience is composed, of course, of those who will receive and benefit from change management training. Whenever possible, we recommend that you provide training for intact work groups, management teams, and change leaders. By training the teams who will work together to implement the organizational change, you can help team members share insights and identify real action steps for getting through the change process. The training session can foster the rapport and team spirit that are crucial during times of transition.

We also recommend that you provide training for management teams. By training whole management teams, you can provide both a safe environment and specific techniques for managers to handle their own concerns and learn the skills they need to guide their employees through organizational changes. By bringing change leaders together, you can raise their awareness of the impact of change on employees and the need to provide appropriate employee training.

Identifying Training Objectives

Your training design will work best if it reflects the current needs and concerns of your organization. In other words, you must meet members of the organization where they are in the change process, before you can help them take the next step. Make sure your design elements match the needs of your participants. For example, if your training audience has just learned of a pending organizational change, your design can focus on helping them deal with their reactions to the change. If your training audience is in the early stages of a major transition, your design can focus on helping them define their long-term goals. If they are deeply involved in implementing a change effort, your design can focus on helping them identify the skills and resources that will get them through the process.

Reinforcing Content

Most trainers of adult learners understand the importance of reinforcing theory with practice—in other words, balancing lecture with experiential learning opportunities. In designing your change management training, it is essential that you include *both* information-rich, didactic presentations *and* interactive, experience-based exercises in your total program.

This book offers exercises designed to support your didactic presentations. By using these experiential activities in your training, you can give participants a chance to apply their learning. For instance, the exercises give learners a chance to think about the process of change, to understand it in a larger context, and to compare their thoughts about change with the thoughts of others. By including the interactive exercises in your training, you can create a "practice area" for employees, managers, and even organizational leaders to feel safe in as they reflect on and deal with their feelings. These activities also offer an excellent opportunity for participants to draw upon their own past experiences with change to help them handle the current situation.

Achieving a balance between lectures and activities in your change management training program requires careful planning. You can select exercises from this book that help reinforce your learning points. The matrix found in the table of contents will assist you with your planning.

Marketing Considerations

Selling Management on the Need for Training

Convincing senior management to invest time and money for change management training in the midst of chaos can be challenging. One of the most effective approaches you can take is to introduce the idea of training long before an organizational change takes place. In this way you can plant the seed, and perhaps obtain management commitment, to make change management training an integral part of any change effort.

As in any marketing effort, your ability to convince management (the buyer) to buy the idea of change management training (the product) depends on how well you (the seller) understand the needs of management. While organizational leaders often know very well how to create change, they may or may not know how to support their staff and employees in implementing the change. By addressing the needs of management first, you can assure yourself the chance to move on to meeting the needs of others in the organization.

Let management know that change management training can help them:

- Understand the inevitability of change.
- Deal with their own reactions to change and develop strategies for dealing with others' reactions.
- Identify positive realistic outcomes for the change process.
- Develop crucial skills for leading their employees through organizational change.

In addition, help both management and prospective participants understand that the benefits of change management training for nonmanagement employees include:

- Equipping people with the skills needed to move through change;
- Providing a safe forum for addressing the personal impact of organizational change; and
- Preparing employees for other, not yet named changes.

Conclusion

Change management training can be one of the most valuable types of training an organization can offer its employees. As changes within businesses and organizations continue to accelerate, leaders and managers who recognize its inevitability and sponsor training to help employees handle change will position their organizations to respond effectively and efficiently. A sample half-day workshop that focuses on preparing managers to lead a change effort follows.

A HALF-DAY CHANGE MANAGEMENT WORKSHOP DESIGN

Audience

12-15 managers

Goal

To prepare managers to lead organizational change.

Objectives

To provide managers with an opportunity to:

- Understand the differences in how people experience and react to change.

- Determine the skills and actions necessary to create the desired organizational culture.

- Discover strategies for reducing potential resistance to change.

- Practice using "hot buttons" as a way of influencing the participation of others in a change effort.

Timing

Total time 4 hours

Workshop Contents

- Introduction
- How do we view change?
- What can we do to bring about positive change?
- How can we handle potential resistance?
- Break
- Do we have to change?
- What skills do I need to bring about positive change?
- How can I influence others constructively?
- What's holding me back from effectively managing change?
- Wrap-Up and Action Planning
- Evaluation

Getting Ready

This half-day managers' training session requires advance preparation. It is important that you, as the trainer and facilitator, familiarize yourself with all instructions and games, copy appropriate handouts, prepare necessary flip charts or overhead transparencies, and assemble required materials.

Preparation before the Training Session

1. Copy (and cut when necessary) the following handouts for each participant:

   - It's in the Cards master set (cut one card for each person) from Game 3.

   - Back to the Future worksheet from Game 26.

   - Strategies for Reducing Potential Resistance to Change sheet from Game 29.

   - Organizational Change Worzle sheet from Part IV.

   - My Hero! My Heroine! worksheet from Game 21.

   - Hot Buttons master set (cut one card for each person) from Game 24.

2. Prepare overhead transparencies or flip charts with:

   - question from step 1 in Game 29.

   - Worzle answer key.

3. Prepare a sample introduction for yourself using a card from It's in the Cards, Game 3.

4. Review all instructions, including those for each game as well as those for the half-day workshop. *Notice that suggested comments for the facilitator are italicized.*

5. Arrange for the room setup using the following guidelines:

   - Have participants sit at small tables (rather than one large U-shaped or other arrangement) to make it easier to break into small groups. Seat 4 to 5 people per table.

   - Make sure required equipment (flip chart, overhead projector, and screen) is in the room before the session begins.

Materials

1. Participant handouts
2. Prepared flip charts or overhead transparencies
3. Overhead projector and screen
4. Transparency markers (if needed)
5. Colored felt-tip markers
6. Pencils
7. Paper (sheets and slips)
8. Trash bag

9. Prize for the Worzle game (optional)

The Day of the Event

1. Make sure the room is set up properly.

2. Greet people as they arrive and make sure they have nametags or tent cards if you are using them.

3. Distribute handouts (at table places or as people arrive).

4. Help participants settle in and find their seats.

5. Let participants know when two minutes remain before the session begins.

6. Ask participants to be seated, then stand in the front of the room.

Trainer-Facilitator Workshop Agenda

Segment	Estimated Time

1. Introduction — 10 minutes

The trainer explains the purpose of the session and reviews the objectives and the agenda.

2. How Do We View Change? — 20 minutes
(Game 3, It's in the Cards)

Participants introduce themselves by completing a statement about change from a prepared card. They discuss their insights about the group's perspective on change based on all responses.

3. What Can We Do to Bring about Positive Change? — 45 minutes
(Game 26, Back to the Future)

Participants complete a worksheet about their current and desired organizational culture, as well as important actions for attaining their goals. They share their ideas first in pairs and then with the full group.

4. How Can We Handle Potential Resistance? — 30 minutes
(Game 29, Wrestling Resistance)

Participants consider individually why they have resisted change in the past, then form small groups to develop strategies to reduce such resistance. Small groups share their strategies with the full group.

5. Break — 15 minutes

6. Do We Have to Change? — 10 minutes
(Organizational Change Worzle)

Participants compete to solve a word puzzle and then discuss their reactions to the change-related words in the exercise, as well as the inevitability of change.

7. What Skills Do I Need to Bring about Positive Change? — 40 minutes*
(Game 21, My Hero! My Heroine!)

Participants focus on someone they admire by completing a worksheet and then sharing in pairs what skills their hero or heroine demonstrated for managing change. They identify the skills they need to bring about positive change in their organization.
*Adaptation of this exercise adds 15 minutes.

8. How Can I Influence Others Constructively? — 30 minutes
(Game 24, Hot Buttons)

Participants form small groups to identify the hot buttons of various audiences in specific circumstances as the first step in influencing those audiences. They generalize their observations to their own organization.

9. What's Holding Me Back from Effectively Managing Change? — 15 minutes
(Game 50, Letting Go for Getting On)

Participants write something down that they need to let go of in order to proceed with desired changes. The trainer collects the papers and ceremoniously discards them.

10. Wrap-Up and Action Planning — 15 minutes

The trainer summarizes the key points of the day and invites participants to share one thing they will do differently as they lead change efforts within their organization.

11. Evaluation — 10 minutes

PARTICIPANT WORKSHOP AGENDA

Introductions

Focus Questions

> How do we view change?
>
> What can we do to bring about positive change?
>
> How can we handle potential resistance?

Break

Focus Questions

> Do we have to change?
>
> What skills do I need to bring about positive change?
>
> How can I influence others constructively?
>
> What skills do I have and what skills can I develop?
>
> What's holding me back from effectively managing change?

Wrap-Up and Action Planning

Evaluation

TRAINER-FACILITATOR WORKSHOP INSTRUCTIONS

Objective

To review the session objectives and agenda.

Time

10 minutes

Setting the Stage

Introduce yourself and welcome participants.

Cover any relevant logistics.

Leading the Activity

State the session goal and review the objectives and agenda.

Answer any questions.

Moving to the Next Segment

Share your enthusiasm about the session.

We have a really full agenda today, so let's get started.

HOW DO WE VIEW CHANGE?

Objective

To understand differences in how people experience and react to change.

Time

20 minutes

Game Used

Game 3, It's in the Cards

Setting the Stage

Tell participants that a good way to start thinking about change is to think about where the group is starting from—where they are now regarding their views of change.

To help us do this, let's introduce ourselves in a way that will highlight how each of us tends to experience and react to change.

Leading the Activity

Follow the directions and debriefing in Game 3, It's in the Cards.

Moving to the Next Segment

Comment that it's easier to move forward when you understand how you view change. Note whether individuals in the group stated similar or different views about change.

WHAT CAN WE DO TO BRING ABOUT POSITIVE CHANGE?

Objective

To determine the actions necessary to create the desired organizational culture.

Time

45 minutes

Game Used

Game 26, Back to the Future

Setting the Stage

Comment that knowing our individual starting points is only one component of creating a desired organizational culture.

You also have to know where your organization is starting from and where you want it to go. Remember: You can only figure out how to get "there" if you know where both "here" and "there" are—where you're starting from and where you're going.

This exercise is designed to help you define "here"—your current organizational culture, and "there"—your desired organizational culture. You'll be able to see what views of the future the group has in common. You'll also have the chance to identify some of the steps or actions you might take to get from "here" to "there."

Leading the Activity

Follow the directions and debriefing in Game 26, Back to the Future.

Moving to the Next Segment

Comment on the clarity of the group's ideas and pictures of where they are starting from, where they are going, and what they need to do to get there.

With such a clear map of the changes needed in your organization, it should be easy to move straight through the change, right?

Pause for group members to comment.

Of course it's not likely to be that easy. What are the chances that there will be no barriers or resistance to your implementation of changes within your organization?

Allow several participants to comment, expecting answers like "Slim," "Impossible," and so forth.

HOW CAN WE HANDLE POTENTIAL RESISTANCE?

Objective

To discover strategies for reducing potential resistance to change.

Time

30 minutes

Game Used

Game 29, Wrestling Resistance

Setting the Stage

It seems it's human nature to resist change, with some of us resisting more often and more strongly than others. In this exercise, you'll have the opportunity to look at ways in which you've resisted change in the past, in order to understand what resistance you might face in your organization. After identifying the reasons for your past resistance, you'll have time to develop some strategies for addressing those reasons in preparation for the months ahead.

Leading the Activity

Follow the directions and debriefing in Game 29, Wrestling Resistance.

Moving to the Next Segment

Comment on the fact that the group has discovered some very practical strategies for reducing potential resistance to change within an organization.

We're going to take a break now. When you come back from the break you'll find a Worzle—a word puzzle—at your seat. The first person or persons to complete the worzle will receive special recognition [or win a prize].

Break

15 minutes

DO WE HAVE TO CHANGE?

Objective

To raise awareness of the inevitability of change.

Time

10 minutes

Game Used

Organizational Change Worzle, Part IV

Setting the Stage

Let participants know when two minutes remain in the break. Remind them that getting back to their seats on time will give them a competitive advantage in completing the Worzle.

Leading the Activity

Follow the directions and debriefing in the Organizational Change Worzle.

Moving to the Next Segment

Comment on how well participants did in decoding the Worzle. Suggest that they now know even more about their attitudes about change.

WHAT SKILLS DO I NEED TO BRING ABOUT POSITIVE CHANGE?

Objective

To emphasize the skills needed to create or implement change.

Time

40 minutes*

*Adaptation to this exercise adds 15 minutes.

Game Used

Game 21, My Hero! My Heroine!

Setting the Stage

Before the break you identified your starting point, where you want to go, and how you can get there. Another key component in implementing successful organizational change is having the right skills to do the job in a way that provides short-term and long-term benefits to the organization. In this exercise, you'll be thinking about the skills that are necessary for leaders of change—like yourselves—to be effective. You'll also be considering which of these skills you already have and which ones you may need to develop.

Leading the Activity

Follow the directions and debriefing in Game 21, My Hero! My Heroine!

Adaptation:

Ask each member to share, and list the skills they mention on the flip chart.

When all of the skills have been listed, briefly review them.

Moving to the Next Segment

Comment on the importance of participants recognizing the skills they already have and the skills they need to develop.

By improving your own skills, you can set a good example for those you manage, perhaps even becoming role models for them. Your willingness to do what it takes to implement desired changes could help others see how important the change effort is to you and to the organization.

HOW CAN I INFLUENCE OTHERS CONSTRUCTIVELY?

Objective

To practice responding constructively to people's "hot buttons" as a way of influencing their participation in a change effort.

Time

60 minutes

Game Used

Game 24, Hot Buttons

Setting the Stage

No matter how well you develop your skills in managing and implementing change, you can't do it by yourselves. Change will only happen when everyone in your organization—or at least a significant number of people—actively participates toward the organization's success.

Comment that because participants will need to involve others in the change effort, they are likely to find themselves in the position of having to persuade or influence some people to join in making changes.

In this exercise, you'll have the chance to practice responding constructively to people's hot buttons—what they react and respond to—as a way of influencing their participation in your organization's change effort.

Leading the Activity

Follow the directions and debriefing in Game 24, Hot Buttons.

Moving to the Next Segment

Comment on the group's identification of many crucial strategies for how to persuade and influence others to contribute to the success of organizational change.

WHAT'S HOLDING ME BACK FROM EFFECTIVELY MANAGING CHANGE?

Objective

To identify what individuals must let go of in order to make a desired change.

Time

15 minutes

Game Used

Game 50, Letting Go for Getting On

Setting the Stage

A final and very important component in creating and implementing change—especially for managers and leaders—is knowing if and when there is something within you that could get in the way of your effectiveness. As you recognize and release any attitudes or reactions that might hinder your success, you will help propel yourselves and your organization through desired changes. In this exercise, you'll have the opportunity to identify and let go of something that might be holding you back from effectively managing change.

Leading the Activity

Follow the directions and debriefing in Game 50, Letting Go for Getting On.

Moving to the Next Segment

This exercise teaches us a good lesson: that improvement is not only about learning new skills or adding knowledge; improvement is also about letting go.

Suggest that participants repeat this process for themselves periodically to make sure they are free from attitudes and reactions that could keep them from being successful change agents in their organization.

WRAP-UP AND ACTION PLANNING

Objective

To give participants a chance to review what they've learned from the session.

Time

15 minutes

Setting the Stage

It's been a full session and we've accomplished a lot.

Summarize what the group covered, including several or all of the following:

- Identified the starting point for change.
- Defined the desired organizational culture.
- Determined action steps for achieving the desired outcome.
- Discovered strategies for overcoming resistance to change.
- Identified necessary skills for leading an organizational change effort.
- Determined ways to influence others constructively to contribute to successful change.
- Assessed individual skills and made plans for developing needed skills.
- Released old or limiting attitudes or behaviors that could have interfered with change.

Leading the Activity

Invite participants to share one thing they learned about themselves or the process of change that will help them to be effective leaders of change in their organization. Accept as many answers as time permits.

Thank everyone for coming and for actively participating in the session. Encourage them to use and build upon what they learned today.

EVALUATION

Objective

To collect data concerning the training program in order to make continuous improvements and upgrades.

Time

10 minutes

Leading the Activity

Ask participants to complete the evaluation forms and return them to you before leaving the training room.

MANAGING ORGANIZATIONAL CHANGE TRAINING EVALUATION

1. What was helpful or most beneficial to you about this training?

2. What could have been better about this session?

3. What other training topics might be addressed in the future?

4. What other comments or suggestions do you have?

Icebreakers
and Openers

1. YOU OUGHTA BE IN PICTURES

Purpose

To recognize that change is an inevitable part of life.

Play Time

30 minutes

Physical Activity

Some

Participation Format

Individuals or unlimited number of groups of 4

Materials and Preparation

11 × 14-inch white sheets of paper (1 for each participant)

Colored felt-tip markers or crayons for drawing

Trainer Notes

Employees often react to the introduction of major change as if change itself were new to them. Consequently, they may resist the change or feel overwhelmed by it, forgetting how many changes they have already experienced in their lives and how natural change is—for both individuals and organizations. As Heraclitus said in 513 BC, "There is nothing permanent except change."

In this exercise, participants have the opportunity to remember themselves as teenagers and consider the many changes that have occurred in their lives since then. With this activity they can remind themselves of the inevitability of change and lessen their resistance to current changes at work.

Directions

1. Instruct participants to take 5 minutes to draw a picture of themselves as teenagers.

2. Give participants 2 minutes to think about at least 1 significant way they have changed since the time of the pictures. Alert participants that they will be sharing this information with other participants.

3. Instruct participants to form groups of 4.

4. Ask participants to take 1 minute each to introduce themselves and share the pictures and the changes that have occurred.

Debriefing

1. At the conclusion of sharing, ask participants:

   - How did you feel about or react to changes?

   - Were you afraid?

   - Did you welcome change? (Link to organizational change taking place.)

   - How many of the changes mentioned were the result of a choice to change?

   - How many were imposed?

   - Did the experience of change differ in the 2 circumstances? (Ask for parallels to changes happening in the organization.)

   - How do "size" and "speed" of change affect the experience? (Again, discuss in the context of organizational change.)

2. At the conclusion of debriefing, comment that change is not always an earth-shattering event. Change is inevitable, and it happens in little ways every day. There is no one, and ultimately no thing, that does not go through change to some degree—even rocks go through a silent metamorphosis over billions of years.

Adaptations and Variations

1. When time is limited or when the activity is conducted in a large group, ask for volunteers to share their pictures and changes.

2. Participants can be asked in advance to bring photographs of themselves as teenagers.

2. METAPHORICALLY SPEAKING

Purpose

To recognize that people experience and react to change differently.

Play Time

25 minutes

Physical Activity

Some

Participation Format

Individuals or unlimited number of groups of 4 to 6

Materials and Preparation

Paper for each participant

Colored felt-tip markers or crayons for drawing

Trainer Notes

While people react differently to organizational change, each person moves through somewhat predictable stages, according to Cynthia Scott and Dennis Jaffe, authors of *Managing Change at Work*. The goal of any change effort, they suggest, is to help people move through the stages of denial, resistance, and exploration and into the stage of commitment. To accomplish this goal, managers must understand employee reactions and provide support to employees throughout the change process. That support includes making themselves available to employees, answering questions, and helping employees envision valuable results for themselves and the organization.

In this exercise, participants have the chance to see the many ways people perceive change. Leaders in the group consider how diverse perspectives create a variety of needs, and how they can meet those needs to further their organization's change effort.

Directions

1. Ask participants to draw a picture that completes the following sentence, using a metaphor from nature: "For me, change is like ... because ...." (Let them know that they will be sharing their metaphors with the group.)

2. Offer an example, such as "For me, change is like riding an ocean wave, because it can be frightening as well as exhilarating."

3. Allow 10 minutes for participants to draw their metaphors.

4. Instruct participants to form groups of 4 to 6.

5. Ask participants to take 1 minute to share their metaphors within the small groups.

Debriefing

1. When debriefing, lead the entire group through a discussion of different reactions to change:

- Ask what similarities or differences they heard in the metaphor statements.

- Mention any patterns you notice. For instance, you might say, "Many of you talked about the exhilaration of change. A few of you mentioned that it is a little frightening or even earth-shattering."

- Ask, "How can you link what you have heard in these metaphors to organizational change?"

2. Additionally, when working with the leaders, emphasize the need to recognize these differences and motivate or lead accordingly. Comment that during a change effort leaders are encouraged to:

- Communicate early, thoroughly, frankly, and often.

- Listen as much as they speak.

- Set an example of resilience, acceptance, and positive thinking.

- Help others see the value in changing—share the vision.

- Let employees be a part of the change process, the decision making, and the goal setting.

Adaptations and Variations

1. When time is limited, ask for volunteers from the large group to share their metaphors.

2. Display the artwork.

3. IT'S IN THE CARDS

Purpose

To understand differences in how people experience and react to change.

Play Time

20 minutes

Physical Activity

None

Participation Format

Unlimited number of groups of 4 to 6

Materials and Preparation

Copy and cut the provided It's in the Cards master set (1 card for each person). The master set contains 24 cards.

Prepare your example for sharing.

Trainer Notes

In his book, *Leading Change in Organizations,* Gary Yukl discusses several different theories of change that each describe the change process as a series of sequential stages through which individuals must pass. Change leaders who recognize that people's reactions to change vary in different stages of the process can help those people move through feelings of loss to a genuine willingness to integrate the change.

This exercise facilitates participants' understanding of the wide variety of reactions that people may have to the same change, depending on the stage of the change process in which they find themselves. It helps create a safe space for employees to learn about the different ways in which people respond to change, hopefully increasing their understanding and tolerance of these differences and encouraging them to support one another through organizational changes.

Directions

1. Give each participant 1 card to be used for introduction.

2. Instruct participants to form groups of 4 to 6.

3. Provide an example of introducing yourself by stating your name and completing the statement for 1 of the cards.

4. Ask participants to take 1 minute each to do the same within the small groups.

Debriefing

1. Ask the participants what insights they have gained from hearing everyone's responses. Possible replies might include that we all respond to change differently and that our responses are as different as we are unique.

2. Ask how participants can apply what they've learned to handling change within their work environment.

3. Emphasize that we all learned at an early age how to respond to change. Our environment, our upbringing, our life experiences, our role models, and our unique personalities and ways of thinking all contributed to our present states of mind regarding change. What many don't realize is how very important our attitude is to surviving change. A productive attitude can enable us to take new directions in our lives; a counterproductive attitude can make us unable to deal with change.

Adaptations and Variations

When time is limited, ask for volunteers from the large group to share their responses.

IT'S IN THE CARDS

When someone imposes change on me, I am most like (name an animal) because…	I handle change in much the same way as (name a famous historical character) because…
For me, change is like: a. winter b. spring c. summer d. fall because…	Faced with needing to make a decision about an impending change, I would be most likely to: a. go on a hike; b. sit by a body water such as the ocean, a lake, or a river; c. hide under the covers with the blinds down; or d. _____ because…
For me, change is like (name a food), because…	If I could wish upon a star, a change I would wish for is … because…

If I could wave a magic wand and change one thing it would be … because…

I believe that all of life's answers can be found:

a. in the library

b. after a few good hours of Monday night football

c. in the shower

d. _____

because…

The book about change with which I identify the most is:

a. *1984*

b. *Huckleberry Finn*

c. *Of Mice and Men*

d. _____

because…

The book about change with which I identify the most is:

a. *Brave New World*

b. *To Kill a Mockingbird*

c. *Passages*

d. _____

because…

The movie about change with which I identify the most is:

a. *The Graduate*

b. *The Grinch That Stole Christmas*

c. *Mr. Holland's Opus*

d. _____

because…

The movie about change with which I identify the most is:

a. *Casablanca*

b. *The Wizard of Oz*

c. *The Big Chill*

d. _____

because…

The song about change with which I identify the most is:

a. "Changes in Attitude"

b. "Dream the Impossible Dream"

c. "Somewhere Over the Rainbow"

d. _____

because…

The song about change with which I identify the most is:

a. "Raindrops Keep Fallin' on my Head"

b. "Eensy Weensy Spider"

c. "Auld Lang Syne"

d._____

because…

Finish this poem and relate it to change:
     "Roses are red,
        violets are blue…."

My greatest lesson learned about change is (was) … because…

Will Rogers said, "Why not go out on a limb? That's where the fruit is." My opinion about this is … because…

Mark Twain said, "A habit cannot be tossed out the window. It must be coaxed down the stairs at step at a time." My opinion about this is … because…

Gelett Burgess said,"If in the last few years you haven't discarded a major opinion or acquired a new one, check your pulse. You may be dead." My opinion about this is … because…

Heraclitus said, "A man can never put his toe in the same river twice." My opinion about this is … because…

John F. Kennedy, Adolf Hitler, and Abraham Lincoln are all known for the impact they had on political change. Of these three, I am most like… because…

Mother Theresa, Martin Luther King, and Nelson Mandela are all known for the impact they had on social change. Of these three, I am most like… because…

Thomas Edison, Orville Wright, and Neil Armstrong are all known for the impact they had on technological advances. Of these three, I am most like… because…

Elvis Presley, Jackie Kennedy Onassis, and the Beatles are all known for the impact they had on fashion changes. Of these three, I am most like… because…

4. YOU'RE IN MY SEAT

Purpose

To demonstrate different reactions, specifically resistance, to unexpected change.

Play Time

25 minutes

Physical Activity

Some

Participation Format

Individual

Materials and Preparation

Requires that tent cards are already in use in the room.

Allow for time in schedule to move name tents around.

Trainer Notes

While any change can spawn resistance, unexpected change can magnify such resistance. In his book, *Managing at the Speed of Change,* Daryl R. Conner asserts that people's perceptions and expectations of change determine their initial level of resistance. He goes on to say that their level of continued resistance depends on how well—or how poorly—they think they can live up to imposed expectations. The best way to address such resistance, according to Conner, is to help people find some advantages in the change, for themselves as well as the organization.

This exercise gives participants a firsthand experience of unexpected change. It helps them witness many different reactions to such a change and understand how natural it is for people to resist it.

Directions

1. During a break, move the participants' name tents so that seating will change.

2. Once most or all people have been seated, ask the group to describe their reactions.

3. If no one seems to notice that the tent cards have been moved, draw attention to that point, or call upon participants by using the "wrong" name in front of them.

Debriefing

1. Ask participants:

   - How is this exercise like organizational change? Responses may include:

     - People often resist even the smallest change.

     - People like to be warned, if possible, about changes.

     - People respond differently to change.

     - Some people can accept change easily.

     - Some people have more control over what happens.

     - Some people want to be asked for their feedback.

   - How does your experience with this exercise help you understand your reaction to change in your organization?

   - What would have made the change easier for you to accept?

   - What might you do differently in implementing change at work based on what you just experienced?

2. When working with leaders, emphasize the need to recognize the differences in the way people react to change and motivate or lead accordingly. Comment that during a change effort, leaders are encouraged to:

   - Communicate early, thoroughly, frankly, and often.

   - Listen as much as they speak.

   - Set an example of resilience, acceptance, and positive thinking.

   - Help others see the value in changing—share the vision.

   - Let employees be part of the change process, the decision making, and the goal setting.

Adaptations and Variations

1. Move name tents on the second or third day of training.

2. Move furniture around instead of name tents, or do both.

5. YOU ARE HERE

Purpose

To recognize that people's reactions to change may be determined by how much change they have experienced.

Play Time

15 minutes

Physical Activity

None

Participation Format

Individual

Materials and Preparation

Copy the provided continuum as a handout or include it in workbook materials.

Trainer Notes

In his book, *Managing Transitions,* William Bridges claims that people who fail to deal appropriately with a specific loss or change are likely to overreact to subsequent losses and changes. The converse may also be true: People who have dealt successfully with past changes may be well-suited to deal with future changes. In other words, how people handled change in the past relates directly to how well they can handle change in the present.

This exercise provides participants with a chance to recall how many changes they have experienced, and to consider how the insights and skills they gained from those experiences might influence their responses to current or proposed organizational changes. It helps them gain awareness about the link between their past and present experiences of change.

Directions

1. Call attention to the continuum and the delineation of "little change," "moderate amount of change," and "great amount of change."

2. Ask participants to indicate, by marking an X on the continuum, the amount of change they have experienced in their lifetimes. This can include both personal and professional change.

3. Invite participants to share where their marks are either during introductions or by asking now for a show of hands.

Debriefing

1. Ask participants what impact the amount of change they have experienced may have on their reactions to organizational change (imposed or otherwise). Possible responses include:

   - Those who have experienced lots of change might like change (e.g., some of the change might have been self-imposed) or might have great coping skills as a result.

   - Change can
     - Be a wake-up call.
     - Give us confidence.
     - Push us to try to do things we think we cannot do.
     - Force us to become more adaptable and resilient.
     - Empower us.
     - Mature us.

2. Emphasize that although we experience different levels of change, our tolerance for it and our attraction to it affect how we respond to it.

YOU ARE HERE CHANGE CONTINUUM

little   moderate   lots of
change   amounts   change
                of change

_____

57

6. I'D LIKE TO GET TO KNOW YOU

Purpose

To understand differences in how people experience and react to organizational change.

Play Time

25 minutes

Physical Activity

None

Participation Format

Pairs unlimited number of groups of 4 to 6

Materials and Preparation

None

Trainer Notes

In his book, *The Survivor Personality,* Al Siebert points out 4 criteria that define survivors. He says survivors are people who have experienced a major crisis or challenge; surmounted the crisis through personal effort; emerged from the situation with previously unknown strengths and abilities; and found value in their experience.

This exercise aims to uncover the stories of employees who have experienced major changes, and to identify role models in the organization who can help others "survive" current or proposed organizational changes. It emphasizes personal insights about how different people perceive and handle change.

Directions

1. Ask participants to select a partner and instruct the pairs to interview each other. Explain that they will introduce their partners to the small group when the interview period is over.

2. Allow 6 minutes in total, giving each person 3 minutes to interview and 3 minutes to be interviewed.

3. Instruct participants to find out the other person's name, a little about the person's job, something about how he or she views change, and his or her experience with organizational change.

4. Instruct participants to form groups of 4 to 6.

5. Ask each participant to spend 1 minute introducing his or her partner to the small group.

Debriefing

1. Ask participants for their insights concerning what has been shared. Responses might include:

- We all do view change differently.

- Some of us naturally resist change and others thrive on it.

- No reactions are right or wrong, just different.

2. Ask participants:

- What common views about change emerged in your group?

- What were some of the differences mentioned?

- How strongly did people feel about change?

- How did you feel about people with different views from yours? With the same view?

- What are some implications from this exercise for going through change in your organization?

3. Emphasize that our responses to change can be as unique as our thumbprints. Our early experiences, our personalities, our ways of thinking, and our early caregivers have all influenced us. No one response to imposed change can be expected, nor do all of us have the same interest in creating change.

Adaptations and Variations

1. When the group is small, ask participants to introduce their partners to the entire group.

2. When time is limited, ask for volunteers to share their responses.

3. Ask people to talk about their hobbies or towns of birth, rather than their jobs.

7. I DID IT MY WAY

Purpose

To reflect on the many different reactions people have to change.

Play Time

20 minutes

Physical Activity

None

Participation Format

Unlimited number of groups of 4 to 6

Materials and Preparation

Copy and cut the provided I Did It My Way master cards (1 card for each person). The master set contains 30 cards. If the entire group is larger than 25, make extra copies of the master set or create additional new cards.

Trainer Notes

In their book, *The Leadership Challenge,* James Kouzes and Barry Posner explore the common practices and commitments of effective leaders. They propose that the single word common to all great leaders is *we,* writing that, "Exemplary leaders enlist the support and assistance of all those who must make the project work. They involve…those who must live with the results. . . ."

This exercise gives participants (the *we* in an organization's change effort) a chance to see how diverse or similar their views of change really are. By identifying the perceptions of those involved in the change, this activity helps leaders to appropriately motivate and involve employees in planned or projected changes.

Directions

1. Distribute 1 card to each participant.

2. Taking 1 minute, provide an example of introducing yourself by stating your name and explaining whether or not the sentence on the card is true of you.

3. Instruct participants to form groups of 4 to 6 and follow your example, including the time limit of 1 minute when introducing themselves.

Debriefing

1. Comment on how different we are in the ways we handle change and mention the fact that no one way of reacting or responding to change is the right way.

   - State that the cards actually reflect statements heard in organizational change management workshops.

   - Comment on the fact that as adults, our many workplace experiences have influenced how we react to change.

2. Mention how exciting and challenging it is that we are so different. We can all learn from one another's perspectives.

3. When working with leaders, emphasize the need to recognize these differences and motivate or lead accordingly.

Adaptations and Variations

1. When the group is small, ask participants to share their responses with the entire group.

2. When time is limited, ask for volunteers to share their responses with the entire group.

I DID IT MY WAY

I do not like surprises.	I love surpirses!
I never met a change I did not like.	I am a change junkie.
For me, change is like being boiled in oil.	For me, change is like a beautiful butterfly emerging from a cocoon.
For me, one change per year is enough.	My coworkers love change, I hate it.
The only changes I can tolerate well are changes in the weather.	Change my $5 bill, not my life.
Change my hairstyle? Yes. Change my attitude? No!	I embrace change.
I look forward to some changes in my life every day.	When things stay the same for a long time, I get very bored.

When things stay the same for a long time, I feel secure.	For me, change is like being caught in a summer rain shower.
Change makes me feel empowered.	It takes me a while, but when I finally decide to make a change … look out!
I cannot sit around and wait for change to happen—I have to look for it.	I know change is going to happen, but I do not search it out … I let it come to me.
I think that with every change there is a buried treasure waiting to be found.	I think that behind every change, there is a poisonous snake waiting to strike.
I believe that if things never changed, the world would be a more peaceful place.	I have to brace myself for change.
When a change is imposed upon me, I meet it enthusiastically.	When I cannot control a change that is happening to me, I become very frustrated and resentful of the change.
I meet change like I would meet an ocean wave.	I dive into change as if I were competing in the Olympics.

For me, change is like getting a chocolate-covered orange cream when I really wanted caramel.	I can always see the light at the end of the tunnel of change.

8. FACT OR FICTION

Purpose

To emphasize the inevitability of changes, even when they seem unlikely.

Play Time

15 minutes

Physical Activity

None

Participation Format

Individual

Materials and Preparation

Copy of Fact or Fiction sheet for each participant

Pencils

Prizes (optional)

Trainer Notes

Because change requires moving from the known to the unknown, it often taps into people's fears. "It's not so much that we're afraid of change or so in love with the old ways," says American futurist Marilyn Ferguson, "but it's that place in between that we fear …. It's like being between trapezes. It's Linus when his blanket is in the dryer. There's nothing to hold on to."

The goal of this exercise is to help participants come to terms with organizational changes, by thinking about the many possible reactions people might have to change and how natural it is to feel discomfort when change occurs. Its design helps people see that even seemingly "impossible" changes can become an integral part of the status quo.

Directions

1. Announce before the break that a Fact or Fiction sheet will be placed at each person's seat just as the break is ending. Encourage participants to return on time to complete their forms, because winners will be determined based on the highest number of correct answers. As the end of the break nears, distribute the sheets.

2. Allow participants 5 minutes to complete the sheets.

3. Review answers with participants, asking for their best guesses. (This can be done immediately following the break or later in the day.)

4. Identify and recognize those with the highest number of correct answers.

Debriefing

1. Ask all participants to identify changes in their lifetimes that seemed nearly impossible or highly unlikely at the time they occurred.

2. Emphasize that if there is one constant in life, it is change. Ironically, there is probably nothing more universal in people than a healthy resistance to change. No matter how certain change is, it rarely feels like a natural occurrence, whether we seek it or it finds us and regardless of whether it is viewed as a positive or a negative change. For instance, people who prefer to communicate via the phone or in person could not imagine communicating any other way. They saw the use of E-mail on a regular basis as an impossibility. Today many of those people who resisted the switch to E-mail are huge proponents and cannot imagine doing business any other way.

FACT OR FICTION

Please read the following statements.

- Circle those that you think were actual predictions in 1893.
- Place a star beside the ones that came true.

_____ An income tax is coming.

_____ Hypnotism will replace anesthetics in surgery.

_____ Homes will be air-conditioned.

_____ The government will set up colleges to train servants.

_____ Women will vote.

_____ Houses and cities will be built of aluminum.

_____ Florida will boom as a leisure state.

_____ Unemployment will disappear.

_____ Cities will become groups of suburbs.

Note: Originally appeared in the May-June 1993 issue of *The Futurist*. Used with permission from the World Future Society, 7910 Woodmont Avenue, Suite 450, Bethesda, MD 20814; (301) 656-8247; http://www.wfs.org/wfs.

FACT OR FICTION ANSWER KEY

All of these statements were 1893 predictions, as cited in *Today Then ...* by Dave Walter.

According to the May-June 1993 edition of *The Futurist* magazine, *all* should be circled and the following should be starred:

★ An income tax is coming.

Hypnotism will replace anesthetics in surgery.

★ Homes will be air-conditioned.

The government will set up colleges to train servants.

★ Women will vote.

Houses and cities will be built of aluminum.

★ Florida will boom as a leisure state.

Unemployment will disappear.

★ Cities will become groups of suburbs.

Note: Originally appeared in the May-June 1993 issue of *The Futurist*. Used with permission from the World Future Society, 7910 Woodmont Avenue, Suite 450, Bethesda, MD 20814; (301) 656-8247; http://www.wfs.org/wfs.

9. YOU ARE A FAMOUS PERSON

Purpose

To acknowledge the differences in the way people handle change.

Play Time

20 minutes

Physical Activity

None

Participation Format

Groups of 4 to 6

Materials and Preparation

Pictures of movie and television stars, cartoon characters, and politicians (1 picture per person)

Trainer Notes

People have different views of change depending on how they are involved in making change happen. In their book, *The Challenge of Organizational Change*, authors Rosabeth Moss Kanter, Barry A. Stein, and Todd D. Jick predict that each person will understand and react differently to what is taking place depending on whether they are planning, carrying out, or just living with the change.

In this exercise, participants have an opportunity to acknowledge different views of change, which may be due in part to the role one plays in making desired changes. In addition, they can learn from each other and expand their perspectives of change.

Directions

1. Give each person 1 picture by putting it in the participant materials at the beginning of a session or distributing them when you need them.

2. Provide 3 to 4 minutes for each person to think about and write down how the person or character on the card handles change.

3. Divide participants into groups of 4 to 6 and have them tell each other what they wrote, allowing 1 minute per person.

4. Call upon 1 person from each group to give 1 or 2 examples from the group.

Debriefing

1. Comment about the wide range of differences in how people—even cartoon characters—react to change.

   - Ask participants:

     - How many of you identified with 1 or more of the characters presented in the group?

     - What can you learn from looking at others' ways of dealing with change, even if those others are cartoon characters?

     - How can these lessons be applied in the workplace?

   - Emphasize that it is true that we can learn from one another's approaches to managing change. We may even try to emulate a person's style or intentionally avoid doing so. The point is to pick and choose what works for us.

2. When working with leaders, emphasize the need to recognize the differences in the way people handle change and motivate or lead accordingly.

Adaptations and Variations

1. Use magazines, newspapers, and worn children's and adult books as a source for the pictures.

2. Collect pictures from the group to reuse for the next group.

3. Make it easier for yourself by using pictures that you find rather than setting out to find specific ones.

10. CHANGE ... NATURALLY

Purpose

To recognize how easily we adapt to changes and how soon they become a natural part of life.

Play Time

20 minutes

Physical Activity

None

Participation Format

Unlimited number of pairs

Materials and Preparation

Paper and pencils for each participant

Trainer Notes

Organizational Transitions by Richard Beckhard and Reuben T. Harris begins by stating that "even the future ain't what it used to be." The authors suggest that organizations in the midst of extraordinary and continuous change must respond quickly and soundly to the myriad of factors that affect them, including new national boundaries, institutions, government regulations, and cultural values and norms.

This exercise gives participants a chance to think about seasonal changes and about how routine such changes have become in their lives. They then discuss what organizational changes have become natural parts of their work experience.

Directions

1. Ask participants to write down the changes that occur when one season changes to the next (i.e., spring to summer, summer to fall, fall to winter, and winter to spring). They should only deal with one season to another, not all the seasonal changes.

   Example (for facilitator understanding): From winter to spring robins return, flowers break through the soil, leaves appear, the temperature warms, the days get longer, baseball gets into swing, road construction projects resume, etc.

2. Next, ask participants to take 5 minutes to record what changes they make or things they do when the season they described is moving in (e.g., do some spring cleaning, start exercising, get outdoors more, donate worn out or unused clothing to someone less fortunate, etc.).

3. Have them share what they have written with 1 other person.

4. Request a few examples for large group sharing.

Debriefing

When debriefing, comment on how inevitable change really is and how naturally we adjust to it. Additionally, comment that adapting to workplace changes can be as easy and natural as adjusting to seasonal changes. This has been especially true of technological changes for some people in the workplace. Ask participants for examples of changes in the workplace that have become a natural part of life.

11. TEAM JUGGLE

Purpose

To emphasize the challenge of managing the complexities of any organizational change.

Play Time

30 minutes

Physical Activity

Moderate

Participation Format

Teams of 10 to 12

Materials and Preparation

4 foam Koosh® balls per team

Activity requires a large training room with adequate space, an empty room, or outdoor space.

Trainer Notes

As Daryl R. Conner maintains in *Managing at the Speed of Change,* people are juggling more tasks, more personal problems, and more opportunities than ever before. Work teams that are dealing with multiple changes often find themselves at many different places in the change cycle at the same time—implementing one change while planning a second and evaluating the completion of a third, for example.

This exercise simulates the speed and complexity of having to face more than one change at a time. It provides participants with an opportunity to discuss how it feels to be in the midst of multiple changes, wondering or worrying whether they might be the one to "drop the ball."

Directions

1. Ask participants to identify 1 change that is going on in the organization currently and the impact of that change on employees.

2. Ask for 3 more changes and impacts.

3. Instruct participants to form teams of 10 to 12 and form 2 lines, which will allow them to toss a ball between the lines, as shown.

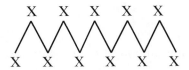

4. Put 4 balls next to the start of each line. Explain that the first player will toss the first ball to the player across from him or her and that player will throw the ball to the next person in the opposite line, until everyone has caught the ball all the way down the line. Participants will toss the ball back to the beginning in the same fashion. Participants must throw the ball to the same 2 people throughout the game. Allow the team(s) to practice for 1 minute.

5. Let the group know that after the first ball has made it up and down the row once, the first person in line will add other balls as instructed. All balls are to be thrown in the same pattern as the first.

6. Announce that the first ball represents the first change (name it) that they identified.

7. After 1 minute ask the first person to add a second ball and name an impact that the group identified. After another minute, ask the first person to add a third ball, which represents another impact. After another minute, add a fourth ball, which represents either an impact or another change. Encourage the group to keep all 4 balls going.

8. Ask participants to return to their seats.

Debriefing

1. When debriefing the activity, ask the participants how this exercise is a metaphor for managing change in their organization. Possible answers include:

   - It was difficult to juggle all these balls, just as it is difficult to manage numerous changes and the impact that those changes have.

   - It takes the whole team to juggle all the balls, i.e., manage all the changes.

   - Juggling (leading change) can be fun. If the group works together as a team, they can do (juggle 4 balls, deal with change) what an individual cannot.

   - Change often comes at people from several directions.

   - The team can fall apart if the ball is dropped (or if 1 person drops the ball).

   - A certain momentum and timing are important.

2. Ask participants:

   - What helped them in doing the exercise?

   - What inhibited them?

   - How can they apply what they've learned to their organization's change effort?

   - What might they do differently in responding to (or handling) change?

3. Summarize the participants' comments.

12. GRAB BAG

Purpose

To creatively marshal resources to manage change.

Play Time

20 minutes

Physical Activity

None

Participation Format

Unlimited number of groups of 4 to 6

Materials and Preparation

Paper and pencils for each participant.

1 bag per group filled with 8 different inexpensive items. Possibilities include, but are not limited to: pencils, chewing gum, hard candy, humorous phone message pads, herbal tea bags, key rings, magnets, and yo-yos.

Trainer Notes

Successfully embracing change depends on a person's ability to identify the options and resources available for managing the effects of an impending change. According to Lillie Brock and Mary Ann Salerno in their book, *The InterChange Cycle*™, an individual should "never say no to a new idea" and should be especially creative during times of change.

The goal of this exercise is to help participants recognize the importance of being open to new ideas and identifying resources during times of change. Additionally, it emphasizes the importance of finding creative options, or "thinking outside the box."

Directions

1. Instruct participants to form groups of 4 to 6.

2. Give each group a filled bag from which to draw items.

3. Give out papers and pencils for brainstorming. Ask each group to select 4 items from the bag. Have groups take 10 minutes to brainstorm how the items selected from the grab bag could help them cope with or manage change.

4. Allow about 8 to 10 minutes for volunteers from each group to share their ideas with the entire group.

Debriefing

When debriefing this activity, remind participants:

- to use brainstorming as a tool in identifying resources;
- to ask for help in identifying resources; and
- to be creative in their use of resources (i.e., never say no to a new idea).

Content-Driven Activities

13. A TRIP DOWN MEMORY CHANGE LANE

Purpose

To broaden participants' perspective on change by focusing on how dramatically life has changed over time and on what drives change.

Playtime

30 minutes

Physical Activity

Some

Participation Format

Groups of 4 to 6

Materials and Preparation

Piece of flip chart paper and marker for each group

Masking tape

1 index card per group containing the name of 1 area listed in step 2 of the directions

Trainer Notes

In their book, *Organizational Transitions,* Richard Beckhard and Reuben T. Harris describe numerous ways that an organization can change, such as by revising the organization's mission, structure, ways of doing business, or culture. Each of these types of change can be driven by the same or different reasons.

In this exercise, participants think about the changes that have occurred over time, and then discuss what drove or inspired those changes. They also have the chance to share their insights about change with each other.

Directions

1. Instruct participants to form groups of 4 to 6.

2. Give each group a card with 1 of the following areas written on it:

Banking/Banks	Gas Stations	Religious Organizations
Education	Cooking	Families
Workplace Communications	Television	Workplace Etiquette
Grocery Stores	Clothes	Women's Roles in the Workplace

3. Ask each group to discuss and record on the flip chart paper how its area has changed over time. Also ask each group to identify the biggest change in the area over time, and to circle that change. Allow 10 minutes for this discussion.

4. Ask each group to post its flip chart and report to the large group what was selected as the biggest change. Encourage everyone to review all the flip charts at the break.

Debriefing

1. Ask participants what conclusions about change they draw from this exercise. Responses might include:

   - A change in 1 area impacts other areas.

   - The rate of change is getting faster.

   - Nothing is exempt from change.

   - We are capable of dealing with a great amount of change.

   - The world has changed a great deal; why should the workplace be exempt?

   - Life is better as a result of change.

2. Ask participants what drove these changes. Responses might include:

   - Customer demands

   - Economic demands

   - Technological demands

   - Attitude demands (bigger, better, faster)

3. Make the points that many of these changes were imposed rather than chosen and that many people prefer the new ways to the old ways.

4. Ask participants how their insights as a result of this exercise can be applied to their experience of organizational change.

5. Summarize the discussion.

Adaptation or Variation

1. Use areas related to participants' industry, geographical location, etc.

14. WE'VE LOOKED AT CHANGE FROM ALL SIDES NOW

Purpose

To reflect on what others need to get through the change process.

Play Time

30 minutes

Physical Activity

None

Participation Format

Groups of 4

Materials and Preparation

Copy and cut 1 set of I Did It My Way cards for each team (from Game 7).

Trainer Notes

Most organizational change theorists agree that many people experience change differently and therefore require varied types of support throughout a change effort. In their book, *The InterChange Cycle*™, Lillie Brock and Mary Ann Salerno identify 2 unpredictable aspects of people's reaction to change: the time and the intensity of their responses. Because there is no way of predicting how long it will take individuals to work through a change or how strongly they will react to that change, it is often difficult to provide effective support.

This exercise offers participants an opportunity to reflect on what people, including themselves, might require to successfully navigate their way through the organization's change process. The goal is to help them understand the challenges associated with meeting diverse and unpredictable needs.

Directions

1. Instruct participants to form groups of 4.
2. Distribute 1 set of cards to each group.
3. Ask participants to take 5 minutes to review all the cards.
4. Instruct participants to choose the card with which they most identify.
5. Direct participants to share with their group which card they chose and why. Tell groups that each participant should take up to 2 minutes to share.

Debriefing

1. Ask participants:

   - How many found similarities among the cards chosen?

   - How many found differences?

   - How many found your views about change were the opposite of someone else's view?

   - What are the implications of these discoveries of an organization going through change? Make the point that we all handle change differently, and that makes organizational change a bit more challenging!

2. When working with leaders, emphasize the need to recognize the differences in how people respond to change and to motivate or lead accordingly. For instance, managers should not assume that everyone has the same needs throughout the change process. This means managers need to ask their employees:

   - What information do you need regarding change in your organization?

   - What resources do you need to implement change?

   - What skills do you need to adapt to changes in your organization?

15. MUSICAL CHAIRS

Purpose

To experience some of the feelings and lessons associated with inevitable or imposed organizational change.

Play Time

30 minutes

Physical Activity

Moderate

Participation Format

Entire group (for groups of 20 or less) or a demonstration group (up to 12)

Materials and Preparation

Chairs (1 per person at game's beginning)

CD or tape; or you can ask participants to sing (See suggested music list.)

CD or tape player

Trainer Notes

Unexpected change can be met with many varied reactions, including shock, denial, and anger. When others impose an unexpected change, it is often and predictably met with resistance. Reducing such resistance requires that people understand the reason for the change and have a desire to make it happen, according to Douglas K. Smith, author of *Taking Charge of Change*. Smith also says that for a change to occur, the people being asked to make the change must see value in the change and possess the skills to carry it out.

This exercise focuses on how it feels to be involved in an imposed change effort. It gives participants a chance to discuss some of the effects of unexpected change and identify ways to handle the sense of loss that often accompanies change.

Directions

1. Ask participants to place chairs in a circle with chairs facing out.

2. Ask each player to stand in front of a chair.

3. Start the music. Instruct players to walk in the same direction around the chairs and sit in the chair closest to them when the music stops.

4. After a few moments, stop the music. All players will have a chair this time.

5. Remove a chair. Start the music again. Wait, then stop the music. When it stops, the players will sit again, leaving 1 person without a chair. Instruct that person to leave the circle.

6. Remove another chair, and continue to start and stop the music, removing a chair each time, until only 1 player remains.

Debriefing

1. Ask the group what in their experience of playing musical chairs is like organizational change. Some possibilities for likening change to musical chairs include:

- Organizational change is often a matter of chance.

- Positions are eliminated.

- Some people still have a chair or job but feel guilty (as survivors in downsizing efforts may feel).

- The complexion of the team changes as people drop out (as in reorganization efforts).

- The person controlling the music and removing chairs is calling the shots (as does the senior management team).

2. Regardless of participants organizational level, remind them that:

- If there is one constant in life, it is change. Ironically, there is probably nothing more universal in people than a healthy resistance to change. No matter how certain change is, it rarely feels like a natural occurrence, whether we seek it or it finds us and regardless of whether it is a positive or a negative change.

- One of the reasons for this is that change brings with it a sense of loss. That is because when change happens, something has ended and something new has begun. Even when the change is viewed as a positive one—the birth of your first child, a promotion, the beginning of an exciting journey—there is undoubtedly some sense of finality.

- We are creatures of habit. Our behavior is set up to stay the same. In fact, it's normal to seek the status quo. Even if it's boring and predictable, our routine is comfortable. That is another reason why change is hard: It shakes up the order of things.

- But change can do a lot for us. It can be a wake-up call to action, it can give us confidence in our abilities, it can give us a chance to try things we may think we can't do, it can help us face our fears head-on, it can force us to become more adaptable and resilient, it is empowering, and it matures us.

3. When working with leaders, emphasize the need to recognize the differences in how people view change and the need to motivate and/or lead accordingly.

Suggested Music List

"Changes"—David Bowie

"I'm Changing"—John Lennon

"Change of Heart"—Harold Adamson

"Change Partners"—an old Virginia Reel

"Changing Partners"—Irving Berlin

"Changes in Attitude"—Jimmy Buffet

"Can't Change Me"—Muddy Waters

"Changing My Tune"—Ira Gershwin

"The World Is Changing Hands"—
Dave Davies

"The Change"—Garth Brooks

"The Times They Are a 'Changing—
Bob Dylan

"Turn, Turn, Turn"—The Byrds

"I'm Not Asking You to Change"—
Herman's Hermits

Adaptations and Variations

1. Any group member with a physical disability should be asked to be involved by making observations about participants' reactions during play, by playing the music, or by singing, for example.

2. Have someone play an instrument.

3. Discuss the lyrics of the songs.

4. Line up chairs in a straight line with every other chair facing the opposite direction. This creates a higher activity level.

16. CONCENTRATION

Purpose

To share personal perceptions of change with other team members.

Play Time

20 minutes

Physical Activity

None

Participation Format

Teams of 2

Materials and Preparation

Copy and cut 2 identical sets of the provided Concentration master cards for each team member (40 cards total for each team).

Trainer Notes

Ned Herrmann, in *The Whole Brain Business Book,* suggests that an organizational change effort is an ideal forum for purposeful creativity. Because people think differently about change, they are able to find a wide variety of creative solutions for moving through a transition from the old to the new. Herrmann also points out that some people will need to move through stages of denial, resentment, discomfort, or anger before such creativity can emerge.

This exercise helps participants understand the different ways people have of thinking about change. It emphasizes that because people view and respond differently to change, their ways of handling change are also likely to be different, leading to an overall organizational response to change that is highly creative and effective.

Directions

1. Divide group into teams of 2. Distribute 2 separate, identical stacks of cards to each team.

2. Instruct 1 person in each team to shuffle the cards and lay them face down in rows, in preparation for 15 minutes of active play time.

3. Ask the first player in each team to turn over any 2 cards, trying to find a matched pair. Explain that if the cards are not a match, they are turned face

down again, and if a match is made, the player keeps the cards and takes another turn.

4. Players continue in turn, concentrating on where cards were turned up. After 15 minutes have elapsed, the team with the most matches wins. Acknowledge all ties.

5. At the end of the game, ask team members to choose the card with which they most identify, and share their reasons with the team.

Debriefing

After the teams have shared, debrief this exercise by asking participants what insights they have gained from hearing all the responses and how the insights might affect their handling of organizational changes. A possible reply might be that we all respond to organizational change differently, which means employees adjust to change at different rates.

CONCENTRATION CARDS

"People do not quit playing because they grow old. They grow old because they quit playing." —Oliver Wendell Holmes	"As human beings we are made to surpass ourselves and are truly ourselves only when we are transcending ourselves." —Huston Smith
"To resist change is like holding your breath— if you persist you will die. We must accept motion, must live with motion, and must know ourselves to be forever moving."—David Meier	"If in the last few years you haven't discarded a major opinion or acquired a new one, check your pulse. You may be dead." —Gelett Burgess
"Before you change your thinking, you have to change what goes into your mind."—Unknown	"People support what they help to create." —Unknown
"Change can come with breathtaking speed, leaving a company on the defensive and in financial trouble when it's forced to catch up." —Gary Goldstick and George Schrieber	"Not everything that is faced can be changed, but nothing can be changed until it is faced."—James Baldwin
"A habit cannot be tossed out the window; it must be coaxed down the stairs a step at a time."—Mark Twain	"Our stomachs quiver at the prospects of change. But today's leaders and managers have no choice."—Robert H. Waterman
"Markets change, tastes change, so the companies and individuals who choose to compete in those markets must change." —Dr. An Wang	"Change is not made without inconvenience, even from worse to better." —Richard Hooker

"A man can never put his toe in the same river twice."—Heraclitus	"Weeping may endure for a night, but joy comes in the morning." —from Hebrew Scriptures
"Progress is not created by contented people." —F. Tyger	"If a window of opportunity appears, don't pull down the shade."—Tom Peters
"Come to the edge, he said. They said, We are afraid. Come to the edge, he said. They came. He pushed them … and they flew." —Guillaume Apollinaire	"It is one thing to learn from the past; it is another to wallow in it." —Kenneth Auchincloss
"It is easier to go down a hill than up, but the view is best from the top."—Arnold Bennett	"Why not go out on a limb? That's where the fruit is."—Will Rogers

17. CHARADES

Purpose

To raise awareness about differences in reacting and responding to self-imposed or organizationally imposed change.

Play Time

60 minutes

Physical Activity

Moderate

Participation Format

2 teams of 8 to 10

Materials and Preparation

Copy and cut provided Charade master cards.

Trainer Notes

Peak performers, according to Erik Olesen, handle change well, survive setbacks, continue to succeed, and appear to lead happy lives. He outlines the successful strategies of peak performers in his book, *Mastering the Winds of Change,* and states that individuals can learn to make changes successfully, whether or not they are in control of the actual change.

In this exercise, participants analyze the responses to change of key characters in various movies, books, and songs as a framework for thinking about their organizational changes. In addition, the activity encourages participants to take responsibility for their own responses to expected, unexpected, and imposed changes.

Directions

1. Divide large group into 2 teams of 8 to 10 people, and pair them against each other.

2. Tell the teams that the player who is "it" indicates whether he or she has a movie, book, or song. To signify a movie title, the player pretends to crank an old-fashioned movie camera; to signify a book the player holds hands open with palms up; and to signify a song, the player pretends to conduct an orchestra. The player should indicate the number of words in the title by holding up the corresponding number of fingers. The player should next indicate which word of the title he or she is addressing by holding up his or her fingers again (1 finger equals first word).

3. Explain that during the game, the player will need to use other gestures such as:

- Tugging on the ear means "Sounds like…"

- A coaxing, come closer motion means the teammates are nearing the answer.

4. Instruct players that they will individually act out their titles using pantomimes and gestures, trying to get their teammates to guess the title. Remind players that the person acting may not speak while teammates call out guesses.

5. Remind teams that each player gets 2 minutes and must sit down if the title is not guessed within 2 minutes. Then the next team takes a turn.

6. Ask teams to designate someone on the opposite team to keep track of the time it takes for an answer to be guessed. The team with the least amount of total time wins.

7. Ask a member of each team to shuffle the cards and distribute 1 to each player, and begin the game with teams alternating turns.

8. Acknowledge the winning team(s).

Debriefing

Debrief this exercise by asking the participants the following:

- How did the characters in the movies, songs, or books react to change? (Example: Maria in *The Sound of Music* reacted enthusiastically by committing herself fully to her new role as governess.)

- What actions did the characters in the movies, songs, or books take in response to imposed change? (Example: Dorothy in *The Wizard of Oz* finds herself in the middle of a strange land. Instead of bemoaning her circumstances, she defines her goal—getting home; she makes a plan; she seeks the resources to help her carry out the plan; and she demonstrates a dogged determination to deal with the imposed change. In the end, she and Toto are able to find their way home to Kansas.)

- How do your examples apply to organizational change? (Example: Both Maria and Dorothy endured the hardships associated with imposed change, didn't retreat or quit, and made the transition successfully.)

MOVIES

Big (Movie)	*The Big Chill* (Movie)
Casablanca (Movie)	*The Graduate* (Movie)
The Grinch That Stole Christmas (Movie)	*Mr. Holland's Opus* (Movie)
On Golden Pond (Movie)	*Pocahontas* (Movie)
Sister Act (Movie)	*Sleepless in Seattle* (Movie)
The Sound of Music (Movie)	*The Wizard of Oz* (Movie)

BOOKS

1984 (Book)	*Animal Farm* (Book)
Brave New World (Book)	*The Grapes of Wrath* (Book)
Huckleberry Finn (Book)	*I Know Why the Caged Bird Sings* (Book)
The Little Prince (Book)	*Of Mice and Men* (Book)
Passages (Book)	*Roots* (Book)
To Kill a Mockingbird (Book)	*War and Peace* (Book)

SONGS

"Blowin' in the Wind" (Song)	"Eensy Weensy Spider" (Song)
"I Heard It through the Grapevine" (Song)	"The Impossible Dream" (Song)
"Over the Rainbow" (Song)	"Raindrops Keep Fallin' on My Head" (Song)

MOVIE DESCRIPTIONS

Big

This story is about a young boy whose wish to become older comes true. After an encounter with a carnival genie, Josh, a 12-year-old boy, wakes up as a 35-year-old man (Tom Hanks). As an adult, Josh is hired by a toy company, where his "youthful enthusiasm" prompts his boss to promote him. In the end, he decides he is not ready for all the changes that the adult world brings him.

The Big Chill

Seven college pals from the 1960s are reunited at the funeral of a friend who committed suicide. Having entered adulthood as nonconformists, most now belong to the establishment. The movie portrays them coming to terms with the changes in their lives.

Casablanca

This movie is a classic love and war story about the struggle between diverse individuals who have sought refuge in Casablanca after fleeing Nazi-occupied Europe during World War II. Humphrey Bogart's character realizes that the war takes precedence over his love for his costar Ingrid Bergman's character. The song "As Time Goes By" is a tribute to enduring, never-changing lovers.

The Graduate

This is the story of a college graduate who spends his first summer out of school being seduced by the wife of his father's best friend. He also falls in love with the woman's daughter. Along the way, he defines his own values. The song by Simon and Garfunkle, "Mrs. Robinson," immortalized the movie, starring Dustin Hoffman and Anne Bancroft.

The Grinch That Stole Christmas

This is an animated television classic. The antagonist, the Grinch, attempts to ruin Christmas for the cheerful Whovills who live in his town. On Christmas Eve, he and his dog dress up as Santa Claus and reindeer and take all of the Whovill's Christmas presents and food. But even after taking the presents, the Grinch realizes that he cannot ruin the spirit of the holiday season.

Mr. Holland's Opus

This is a story of a gifted musician who dreams of composing one truly memorable piece of music. To support his family, Mr. Holland takes a job as a high school music teacher and spends most of his life teaching music. Mr. Holland is blessed with a son, but to his dismay, the son is deaf. As their relationship evolves, Mr. Holland realizes that his son can appreciate music. This realization causes him to assert that his real passion is teaching. He realizes his legacy to the generations of young people is not just the experience of music lessons, but also life lessons.

On Golden Pond

This story deals with conflict among three generations. Norman, the cranky but lovable grandfather, is preoccupied with death and emotionally distant from his daughter, Chelsea. He and his wife return to spend their 48th summer on Golden Pond. Starring Kathryn Hepburn and Henry Fonda in Henry's last movie appearance before his death, this movie focuses on the changing relationship between father and daughter. It also focuses on the older couple's dealing with the changes in their lives.

Pocahontas

Pocahontas, the free-spirited young daughter of Chief Powhatan, wonders what adventures await her. In sails the gold-loving Governor on a ship that is full of English settlers, led by the courageous Captain John Smith. A chance meeting between Captain Smith and Pocahontas leads to a friendship that will change history as the American Indians and the English settlers learn to live side by side.

Sister Act

This hilarious comedy film stars Whoopi Goldberg as a lounge singer who is hiding from the mob. She discovers a very unlikely but safe hideout in a convent, where she soon turns the rather pathetic choir into a group of swinging nuns belting out the best of 1960s Motown music.

Sleepless in Seattle

This love story begins when a widowed father, Sam (Tom Hanks), becomes a guest on a radio call-in show. A Hollywood romance writer (Meg Ryan), engaged to be married, decides that she must meet him and goes to Seattle. This story is modeled after the classic movie, *An Affair to Remember*, starring Deborah Kerr and Cary Grant. *Sleepless in Seattle* ended with Tom Hanks and Meg Ryan finally meeting at the top of the Empire State Building.

The Sound of Music

This is a classic musical starring Julie Andrews and Christopher Plummer. Unsure of whether or not to become a nun, Maria (Julie Andrews) takes a job as a governess of seven children whose mother has died. Together, Maria and the children have various adventures. In the end, Maria marries the children's father, an ex-navy captain.

The Wizard of Oz

Caught in a tornado, 12-year-old Dorothy and her dog, Toto, land over the rainbow in the world of Oz, where they meet good and bad witches and munchkins. Throughout the adventure, Dorothy and Toto make new friends: the Tin Man, who lacks a heart; the Scarecrow, who lacks a brain; and the Lion, who lacks courage. In hopes of acquiring their missing parts (a home, a heart, a brain, and courage), Dorothy and her friends set out in search of the mighty Wizard. Dorothy hopes that the Wizard can grant her wish to return home to Kansas.

BOOK DESCRIPTIONS

1984

Published in 1949, this book offers political satirist George Orwell's nightmare vision of a totalitarian, bureaucratic world. It is a story of one man's attempt to discover his individuality.

Animal Farm

This political fable is based on the events of Russia's Bolshevik Revolution and the betrayal of the cause of Joseph Stalin. Barnyard animals overthrow and chase off their exploitative human masters and set up an egalitarian society of their own. Eventually the pigs lead a revolution, forming a dictatorship worse than they had with their former human masters.

Brave New World

In the Utopia described, everyone consumes daily grams of soma to fight depression, babies are born in laboratories, and the most popular form of entertainment is a "Feelie," a movie that stimulates the senses of sight, hearing, and touch. But Bernard Marx feels something is missing and senses his relationship with a young woman could be much more than it is. Huxley wrote about many of the practices and gadgets that we take for granted today.

The Grapes of Wrath

This story describes the survival of the Joad family in California during the Great Depression of the 1930s. As migrant farm workers hoping for rich earth and good jobs, they instead compete for slave wages and live in horrible conditions. They also deal with the hatred and violence of locals frightened by the influx of outsiders. They learn not to question the law for fear of being beaten or run out of town. They band together, hoping for better fortune around the corner.

Huckleberry Finn

Huck experiences adventures on the Mississippi River with an escaped slave, Jim. Huck lives happily, free as a bird, enjoying life on the river.

I Know Why the Caged Bird Sings

This book is the unforgettable memoir of an African American girl recalling the anguish of growing up in the 1930s and 1940s. She lived her teen years in the slums of a tiny Arkansas town.

The Little Prince

This book describes the adventures of a little prince who visited Earth from his own tiny planet. Although whimsical in its approach and full of fantasy, it is a solid look at human values.

Of Mice and Men

This classic story of loyalty and friendship focuses on two traveling farm workers, George and Lennie. George has taken on responsibility for the mildly retarded Lennie, who constantly seems to fall into trouble of one sort or another. George and Lennie do not plan to travel forever, however, and hope to someday have a little place of their own.

Passages

This book describes the predictable and inevitable stages of adult life in our 20s, 30s, 40s, and 50s. The author, Gail Sheehy, outlines the crises we can expect, suggesting opportunities for creative change and problem solving.

Roots

This is a story that traces seven generations of black slaves in America. It reveals the cruelty of humanity.

To Kill a Mockingbird

This is the story of a young girl in Alabama in 1930. Her father, a lawyer, defends an African American accused of raping a white woman. The people of the town are very prejudiced and prone to violence. The young girl sees the impact her father's heroism has on her and the town as he fights for justice.

War and Peace

This book relates war between nations to quarrels between people. It points out that we must overcome individual selfishness if there is to be any hope for peace in the world.

SONG DESCRIPTIONS

"Blowin' in the Wind"
(Lyrics—Bob Dylan)

Bob Dylan's song encourages people to reflect more closely on the significance of life and to go beyond simple, comfortable, or conventional thinking. He encourages us to listen to the "answers in the wind." This song is often associated with social change in the 1960s and 1970s.

"Eensy Weensy Spider"
(An English Folk Song)

This children's song does a delightful job of reminding us of the need to "bounce back" from rough times with strong spirit and commitment.

"I Heard It Through the Grapevine"
(Performed by Creedence Clearwater Revival)

The power of the grapevine for spreading news can be greater than most of us realize, especially when it comes to organizational change. Perhaps, as the song suggests, we need to confirm what we hear.

"The Impossible Dream"
(Lyrics—Joe Darion)
(Music—Mitch Leigh)

This is a song about courage and commitment. It's about knowing what's right and never giving up until you change things for the better. It acknowledges that the effort can seem overwhelming but, because the gains are so great, we should never quit striving to create a better world.

"Over the Rainbow"
(Lyrics—E.Y. "YIP" Harburg)
(Music—Harold Arlen)

Performed by Judy Garland in *The Wizard of Oz,* this is a song about finding peace and happiness. The lyrics suggest that perhaps there is a heavenly place where no troubles exist and where dreams come true. Surely we can create the changes needed to find that internal peace and happiness here on earth.

"Raindrops Keep Falling on My Head"
(Lyrics—Hal David)
(Music—Burt Bacharach)

This song describes the positive attitude we need in order to meet life's challenges. It suggests that complaining, worrying, and crying only serve to defeat us. The freedom to take control and make our lives better is within us.

18. TWENTY QUESTIONS

Purpose

To explore the effectiveness of well-known people in handling change (and learn how their approaches can help us handle today's organizational changes).

Play Time

30 minutes

Physical Activity

None

Participation Format

Groups of 3

Materials and Preparation

Copy and cut the provided Twenty Question master cards. The master set contains 20 different cards.

Trainer Notes

In their book, *The InterChange Cycle*™, Lillie Brock and Mary Ann Salerno explain that people who successfully manage change share a common set of attitudes, beliefs, and skills. For example, they believe that change is a natural part of life; they are confident in their own inner resources to handle change; and they have a clear picture of the results of each change.

In this exercise, participants have the chance to reflect on how well-known people have handled change and learn how they can conduct successful change efforts in their own organization. The exercise highlights the attitudes, beliefs, and skills necessary to make change happen, and hopefully will inspire participants to acquire or adopt these common characteristics.

Directions

1. Divide participants into groups of 3. Designate 1 person per group to be "it" first.

2. Instruct participants to place a name on "it's" back. Tell the person who is "it" to ask up to 20 yes or no questions to guess the identity of the name on the card. (For example: Am I living? Am I male? Did I invent something?)

3. Stop the games when at least 2 people per group have been "it," or when a predetermined time limit is reached.

Debriefing

When debriefing, facilitate discussion with the group about what famous persons can teach us about change. (See provided Background Information Sheets on famous people featured on the Twenty Questions cards.) Questions you might ask include:

- What did the famous people encounter that had to be overcome?
- What skills or resources did they use to achieve their accomplishments?
- How did they respond to change?
- What role did they play in making change happen?
- What qualities did they have in common as they dealt with change?
- How is our opinion of these people related to their roles as change agents?
- Which one would you like to emulate when it comes to implementing change? Why?
- Which person would participants choose to lead the change in their own organization? Why?

TWENTY QUESTIONS

Neil Armstrong	Napolean Bonaparte
Cleopatra	Christopher Columbus
Amelia Earhart	Thomas Edison
Judy Garland	Adolf Hitler
Helen Keller	John F. Kennedy
Martin Luther King Jr.	Abraham Lincoln
Nelson Mandela	Richard Nixon
Elvis Presley	Mr. Rogers
Dr. Benjamin Spock	Mother Theresa
Oprah Winfrey	Orville Wright

BACKGROUND INFORMATION SHEETS

NEIL ARMSTRONG

Neil Armstrong, commander of Apollo 11, was the first person to set foot on the moon. His famous words were, "That's one small step for man, one giant leap for mankind."

Born in Wapakoneta, Ohio, Neil Alden Armstrong knew early in life that he wanted a career in aviation. He learned to fly early getting his pilot's license at age sixteen. He flew jets based on an aircraft carrier in the Navy, and was an engineer, test pilot, astronaut, and administrator with the National Aeronautics and Space Administration (NASA).

After leaving his NASA position, Armstrong was a professor of aerospace engineering at the University of Cincinnati. He currently delivers motivational speeches based on his knowledge and insights gained by his astronaut training and his space missions.

He is also currently chairman of AIL Systems, Inc., an aerospace electronics manufacturer.

NAPOLEON BONAPARTE

Napoleon Bonaparte was born to a poor family on the island of Corsica. He went to French schools because France had annexed Corsica in the year before he was born.

The history of France and Europe during the period from 1799 to 1815 is largely the story of Napoleon Bonaparte. He became a French military officer, rising rapidly to the rank of general. He was placed in command of French forces in Italy and won brilliant victories there. He became quite a hero.

He provided the French people with an efficient system of government and accomplished many legal, administrative, religious, and educational reforms.

Between 1805 and 1807 he defeated Austria, Prussia, and Russia. His ability and power gradually declined, and his disastrous invasion of Russia in 1812 marked the actual beginning of his fall. Defeated at Waterloo in June 1815, Napoleon was exiled to St. Helena, where he died in 1821.

CLEOPATRA

Cleopatra (69–30 BC), Queen of Egypt and daughter of Ptolemy XII, was one of the most fascinating women of all time. She was both intelligent and beautiful. Cleopatra came to the throne in 51 BC, only to be exiled three years later.

Caesar appeared in Egypt in pursuit of his rival, Pompey. When Cleopatra heard that Caesar was in the palace in Alexandria, she rolled herself up in a rug and asked an attendant to carry her to Caesar as a gift. Captivated by her charm, the fifty-two-year-old Roman helped her regain her throne. Ptolemy XIII was drowned and Caesar made Cleopatra's younger brother, Ptolemy XIV, joint ruler with her.

Cleopatra had a son, said to be Caesar's, called Caesarion, meaning "little Caesar." When Caesar returned to Rome, she followed him with the baby and lived in Caesar's villa, where he visited her constantly. After Caesar was assassinated in 44 BC, Cleopatra returned to Egypt. Soon after, Ptolemy XIV died, perhaps poisoned by Cleopatra, and the queen named her son Caesarion coruler with her as Ptolemy Caesar.

Following Caesar's assassination, the Roman Empire was divided. Mark Anthony summoned Cleopatra, assuming she had aided his enemies. She charmed Mark Anthony, and they spent a winter together.

Anthony married Octavia, although he loved Cleopatra, whom he later also married. Octavian (Octavia's sister) was angry and declared war on Cleopatra. Cleopatra took refuge in a mausoleum that she had built for herself. Anthony, who had three children with Cleopatra, was told she was dead and stabbed himself. When he heard that she was actually still alive he asked to be carried to her. He died in her arms and she later committed suicide.

CHRISTOPHER COLUMBUS

Christopher Columbus, a self-educated, Italian-born navigator who sailed in the service of Spain's Queen Isabella, is commonly known as the "discoverer" of the New World, America. A new era of European discovery began with his voyages to the New World. Columbus was actually searching for a new westward route to Asia, which he never found, although the discoveries he did make were even more valuable.

Columbus voyaged in the Mediterranean. He married in 1479, but his wife died shortly after their son, Diego, was born in 1480. By this time, Columbus had become interested in westward voyages, and spent several years trying to get funding for voyages to Asia. Eventually Isabella did fund some expeditions, hoping Columbus would return with gold.

After his first voyage Columbus did return with gold, artifacts, and some Indians. On his second voyage, he set up a colony called Isabella. The colony was later moved and renamed Santo Domingo, and became the first European settlement in the New World. The third voyage brought Columbus to Trinidad and then to the mainland, and thus the discovery of South America. His fourth voyage ended in disaster when Columbus was marooned for a year in Jamaica.

Columbus believed until his death that he had reached Asia. His real greatness lies in the fact that having found the West Indies, even while making major errors in navigation, he was able to find his way back to Europe and back again to the Indies. Because of this, the New World became part of the European world.

AMELIA EARHART

Amelia Earhart died mysteriously at the age of forty. In June 1937 she and her copilot, Lieutenant Commander Fred J. Noonan, left Miami, Florida, on an around-the-world flight attempt in a twin-engine Lockheed aircraft. On July 2 the plane vanished near Howland Island in the South Pacific. The world waited with fascination as search teams from the United Sates Army and Navy, along with the Japanese Navy, converged on the scene. But neither Earhart, Noonan, or the plane were ever found. Historians have claimed that she was almost certainly forced down by the Japanese and killed.

In the last decade of her life, Amelia Earhart became the best-known female aviator in the world. After working as a military nurse in Canada during World War I, she was a social worker in Boston. She gained fame in 1928 when she became the first woman to fly across the Atlantic Ocean, as a passenger. Four years later she made a solo flight across the Atlantic and several solo long-distance flights in the United States.

Earhart took an active role in opening the field of aviation to women. Her publisher and husband, George P. Putman, wrote her biography, *Soaring Wings*, following her disappearance.

THOMAS EDISON

Thomas Alva Edison was born in Milan, Ohio in 1847. At a very young age he suffered hearing loss from scarlet fever; eventually he became totally deaf in one ear and had only ten percent hearing in the other. At 10 years of age, his mother removed Thomas from school and educated him at home, where, because of his love for chemistry, he set up a laboratory. Two years later Thomas moved the laboratory to an empty railcar on the Grand Trunk Railway.

Over the years Thomas became proficient on the telegraph and served as a telegrapher from the southern United States to Canada. As he worked to improve the telegraph, he invented the automatic telegraph, the duplex telegraph, and the message printer. These inventions led to a career as a full-time inventor.

Edison married Mary Stilwell in 1871 and they had three children. Mary's father helped him to build a new lab in Menlo Park, NJ, where he invented the carbon-button transmitter and the cylinder phonograph. With J.P. Morgan's help, Edison opened the Edison Electric Company.

In 1879, he invented the incandescent light bulb. In 1883, an engineer in Edison's lab made a discovery that led to the electron tube. This discovery was patented as "the Edison Effect."

Following the death of his wife Mary in 1884, Edison married Mina Miller in 1886 and together they had three more children. Throughout their years together, he patented many more inventions. By his death in 1931, he had a total of 1,093 patents.

JUDY GARLAND

Judy Garland was born Frances Ethel Gumm in June 1922 in Grand Rapids, Minnesota. She was the third of three girls in the Gumm family. She got her singing start at two-and-a-half years old, at a Christmas show at her parents' theater. The three sisters became known as the Gumm Sisters, and appeared at theaters and social functions in and around Grand Rapids.

A well-known comedian, George Jessel, introduced the Gumm Sisters to an audience, heard the quiet laughter about their name, and suggested that they change to "Garland" from "Gumm." Frances took the name Judy shortly after.

In her short lifetime of 47 years, Judy Garland made 32 feature films, did voice-over work for two more, and appeared in at least half a dozen short subjects. She received a special Academy Award and was nominated for two others. She starred in 30 of her own television shows and appeared as a guest on nearly 30 more. She won a special Tony Award for the first of three record-breaking Broadway engagements at the Palace Theater in New York. She recorded nearly 100 singles and over a dozen record albums, one of which received five Grammy's in 1962 (*Judy at Carnegie Hall*). She performed several hundred radio broadcasts and made personal appearances for the military and for charities.

In 1969, Judy Garland died of an accidental overdose of sleeping pills, which she used to counteract the diet pills she took during the day.

ADOLF HITLER

Adolf Hitler was born in 1889 in Braunau am Inn, Austria. His mother died when he was eight and his father died when Adolf was sixteen. At eighteen he moved to Vienna, Austria. He acquired two convictions there, one for taking a defiant nationalist stance on German pride, and another for virulent anti-Semitism.

Hitler was overjoyed at the start of World War I, and soon volunteered for the German army. He rose to the rank of corporal and was twice awarded the Iron Cross. He was injured twice.

Hitler joined the German Workers Party in 1919, a group that believed the Germans were a master race and the Jews and Communists threatened their purity. They were later renamed the National Socialist Party (abbreviated, the NAZI party). In 1933, President von Hindenburg appointed Hitler Chancellor of Germany. Paul von Hindenburg's death led Hitler to full power, and he peacefully annexed Austria and Czechoslovakia to acquire more land.

In 1933, Hitler took away the right of Jews in Germany to vote. In 1935, he oversaw the passage of the Nuremberg Laws, which stated that Jews and Germans could not marry or do business with each other. In 1940, the Holocaust began, and by 1942, 2.5 million Jews had been killed.

When Germany began to lose the Second World War, Hitler and his wife of one day, Eva Braun, committed suicide.

HELEN KELLER

Born healthy, Helen Keller was struck with an illness at nineteen months of age that left her deaf, blind, mute, and unable to communicate except through violent expressions of her mood. Her family felt unable to help or control her, and until early childhood, Keller knew little more than a world of darkness and the touch and smell of her mother and father.

Anne Sullivan, a young teacher who worked with the blind, heard of Helen and came to live with the Kellers. Partnering with Sullivan, Keller overcame her disabilities. Sullivan patiently worked with Keller, trying to help her make a connection between manual sign language and the object Keller was feeling in her hand. After making that important leap, Keller learned rapidly, reading braille and writing with a special typewriter. At the age of ten, she learned to speak.

Keller set her sights on college, and after graduating cum laude from Radcliffe in 1904, she began lecturing, writing, and fund-raising on behalf of the handicapped. In 1920, she helped to found the American Civil Liberties Union, which was organized to defend the civil liberties of all citizens.

Not only was Keller able to overcome and adapt to her adversities, she also indirectly educated twentieth-century scientists and doctors, who before would not have believed a person with Keller's disabilities could function or even live outside of an institution. Keller changed our outlook on the capabilities of the disabled. Thanks to her dedicated efforts, she also paved the way to reform of the atrocious medical facilities available to challenged persons.

JOHN F. KENNEDY

John Fitzgerald Kennedy was born in 1917 in a suburb of Boston. He was the second of nine children of Joseph and Rose Kennedy. He attended Harvard University, where he majored in government and international relations.

Kennedy became a U.S. Navy seaman when he enlisted after graduating from college. He was involved in Pearl Harbor and was awarded a Purple Heart. His political life began in 1946 when he ran for the U.S. House of Representatives and won. He was reelected several times. In 1953 he married Jacqueline Bouvier, daughter of the wealthy John V. Bouvier III, a Wall Street broker. Their children, Caroline and John F. Kennedy, were born in 1957 and 1960, respectively.

When Kennedy took office, cold war tension between Communist and Western nations was increasing. He pledged strong efforts to halt the spread of Communism. He created the Peace Corps of Young Americans to work in underdeveloped countries. When the Soviets launched the first astronaut into space in April 1961, Kennedy moved the U.S. into the "space race." In the spring of 1961, the Bay of Pigs near Havana, Cuba was invaded by opponents of Cuba's Communist premier, Fidel Castro. Our CIA had aided that invasion, with Kennedy's approval, for which he was later criticized.

President Kennedy was active as an advocate of equal rights. In 1961, a group of black and white freedom riders entered Montgomery, Alabama by bus to test local segregation laws. Riots resulted and Kennedy sent U.S. marshals to the city to help restore order.

In 1963, Kennedy and his wife rode through Dallas in a motorcade. At 12:30 p.m. on November 22, three shots were heard and the President slumped in his seat. Attempts to save him failed. Lee Harvey Oswald was arrested for his murder. Jack Ruby killed Oswald when he was taken from the county jail. The Kennedy assassination has remained a source of controversy over the years.

MARTIN LUTHER KING

Rev. Dr. Martin Luther King, Jr. fought for full citizenship rights for the poor, disadvantaged, and racially oppressed in the United States.

In 1954, King became the minister at his first church in Montgomery, Alabama. Before he and his wife, Coretta, had been there a year, Mrs. Rosa Parks made history by defying the segregation ordinance on city buses. King co-organized the Montgomery bus boycott, which lasted a year, and from that point on he was known nationally as a leader of the Civil Rights Movement.

King followed and further developed Gandhi's nonviolent disobedience doctrine. In 1963, he organized the march on Washington, D.C. where he delivered his famous "I Have a Dream" speech, in which he "subpoenaed the conscience of the nation before the judgment seat of morality." In 1964, King was selected as *Time* magazine's first black Man of the Year. Later that year he also became the youngest recipient of the Nobel Peace Prize. King called for a "reconstruction of the entire society, a revolution of values," as he began to make a connection between racism and poverty.

Early in 1968, while organizing a multiracial poor people's march on Washington, King flew to Memphis to help with a laborers' strike. On April 4th, he was assassinated in Memphis. In 1983, King's birthday, January 15, was designated a national holiday.

ABRAHAM LINCOLN

Abraham Lincoln is considered by many to have been the greatest U.S. president. He is best known for guiding the country through the Civil War and ending slavery.

Raised on a farm, Lincoln received little formal education. After a brief military stint, he entered politics and was elected to the Illinois legislature for four successive terms. Early on he voiced his belief in the American system of economic opportunity, and stated that he did not believe slavery had a place in that system.

Lincoln became a lawyer in 1836, built a successful practice, married Mary Todd, and served one term in the House of Representatives. He stayed involved in politics and, in 1860, was elected the sixteenth U.S. president. In April of 1861, the Civil War began. Lincoln was soon known for taking aggressive measures, sometimes seeming to be in opposition to both the Constitution and his military commanders. The Emancipation Proclamation was possible in part because of his interpretation of the Constitution; he took the position that the Commander in Chief could abolish slavery as a military necessity.

When Lincoln won the 1864 presidential election, Southerners who had just lost their fortunes were frustrated and enraged. Lincoln was shot by Southern-sympathizer John Wilkes Booth, and died on April 15, 1865, only six days after Lee's surrender to Grant at Appomattox.

In his Gettysburg Address of 1863, Lincoln had defined the Civil War as a rededication to the egalitarian ideals of the Declaration of Independence; in his second inaugural address he urged "malice toward none" and "charity for all" in the peace to come.

NELSON MANDELA

Nelson Rolihlahla Mandela was born in South Africa in 1918. He came to be widely accepted as the most significant black leader in South Africa, and a world-wide symbol of victory against apartheid.

Early in his life, in order to pursue a political career, Mandela gave up his right to succeed his father as chief of the Tembu Tribe. He was educated at the University of Fort Hare and the University of Witwatersrand in law. In 1944 he joined the African National Congress. He was tried for treason because he engaged in resistance against the National Party's apartheid policies. He was later acquitted.

Mandela became a fugitive in the early 1960s, but was caught and jailed in 1962. As his reputation grew, a campaign to free him intensified. Set free in 1990, he shared the Nobel Peace Prize with South Africa's president, F.W. de Klerk, for their peaceful struggle for a nonracial democracy.

RICHARD NIXON

Richard Nixon was born in Yorba Linda, a farming village in Orange County, California, in 1913. He became the thirty-seventh President of the United States, serving from 1969 to 1974. His victory followed two previous defeats, one in his bid for the 1960 Presidency (John F. Kennedy became president) and one for the governorship of his home state of California in 1962.

In 1969, Nixon was the first president since the start of the two-party system to assume office with a Congress that opposed him. Renominated in 1972, Nixon enjoyed a landslide victory.

During his time in office, Nixon worked hard on world stability. He reduced tensions with China and the U.S.S.R. His summit meetings with Russian president Brezhnev produced a treaty to reduce strategic nuclear weapons. In 1973, Nixon announced an accord with North Vietnam to end American involvement in Indochina. In 1974, Henry Kissinger, his Secretary of State, negotiated disengagement agreements between Israel and its opponents, Egypt and Syria.

Nixon's administration was embattled over the Watergate scandal. Officials of the Committee to Reelect the President broke into the offices of the Democratic National Committee during the 1972 campaign. Faced with impeachment, Nixon announced on August 8, 1974 that he would resign the next day to begin "that process of healing which is so desperately needed in America."

By the time of his death in 1994, Nixon had gained respect as an elder statesman and had written numerous books about his experiences.

ELVIS PRESLEY

Elvis Presley dominated popular music in the United States after the release of his first big record, "Heartbreak Hotel," in 1956. Forty-five of his records sold more than a million copies each. He made 33 motion pictures and appeared on television and in live concerts, soon becoming the highest-paid performer in show business history. His hip gyrations, thought by some to be sexually suggestive, earned him the nickname, "Elvis the Pelvis."

Drafted into the Army in 1958, Presley went through regular training and then served as a truck driver in West Germany until his discharge in 1960. Resuming his career under Colonel Tom Parker's supervision, Presley worked up a touring act, based in Las Vegas, Nevada, and attracted an ever-expanding public. He bought Graceland, his lavish Memphis mansion, using it as a retreat from the public. In 1967 he married Priscilla Beaulieu. The couple, who had a daughter the following year, were divorced in 1973.

Unable to go anywhere without being mobbed by fans, Presley became increasingly reclusive. He resorted to taking various prescription drugs. He died of heart failure in Memphis on August 16, 1977.

MR. ROGERS

Fred McFeely Rogers, known to most as Mister Rogers, was born in 1928 in La-trobe, Pennsylvania, a small town east of Pittsburgh. Following his education at Rollins College in Florida, where he majored in music, Rogers was hired by NBC in New York as an assistant producer. In 1952, he married Joanne Byrd, a pianist and a fellow Rollins graduate.

When WQED, the nation's fist community-supported public television station, ap-proached Rogers for help in 1953, he moved back to Pittsburgh. Rogers was to develop program schedules for the following year. One of the shows, *The Chil-dren's Corner,* won the Sylvia Award as the best locally produced children's pro-gram in the country. While he worked with *Children's Corner,* Rogers began study-ing child development and attended the Pittsburgh Theological Seminary. He was ordained in 1962.

Rogers appeared on camera for the first time as a program host in Toronto in 1963, where he created a 15-minute children's series called *Mister Rogers.* He came back to Pittsburgh and expanded the 15-minute segments to a half-hour format; by 1968 the series was available to affiliates of the Public Broadcasting Service.

Rogers was appointed chairman of the Forum on Mass Media and Child Develop-ment of the White House Conference on Children and Youth. Among other awards, he received two George Foster Peabody Awards and several Emmy's. He is chairman of the Board of Family Communications, Inc., a nonprofit corporation that produces materials to encourage the healthy emotional growth of children and their families. After several decades of production, *Mister Rogers Neighborhood* is still a place focused on the growth of children.

DR. BENJAMIN SPOCK

Benjamin Spock influenced several generations of parents in the United States. His book, *The Common Sense Book of Baby and Child Care,* was translated into 39 languages and was an all-time best seller, second only to the Bible in sales. Spock encouraged parents to trust and respect themselves and to listen to their children. He focused on the needs of children rather than the convenience of parents.

Spock was also known for his involvement in the peace movement. He was concerned about the issue of nuclear testing. He was also an outspoken critic of the Vietnam War.

Besides his best seller, he wrote *Dr. Spock Talks with Mothers* (1961), *Problems of Parents* (1962), *Caring for Your Disabled Child* (1965; in collaboration), *Raising Children in a Difficult Time* (1974), and *Decent and Indecent: Our Personal and Political Behavior* (1970).

Despite earning millions of dollars in book royalties, Spock and second wife, Mary Morgan, forty years his junior, experienced financial problems because of his deteriorating health. Dr. Benjamin Spock died in 1998.

MOTHER THERESA

Mother Theresa, winner of the 1979 Nobel Peace Prize, dedicated her life to serving Calcutta's homeless poor. She founded a Roman Catholic order of nuns to expand her work, and established leper colonies and homes for the dying.

Born in Albania with the name Agnes Gonxha Bejaxhiu, she entered the order of the Sisters of Our Lady of Loreto at the age of 18. She taught in the order's school in Calcutta until 1946, when she experienced a call to aid the poor of India.

Mother Theresa began her work by bringing dying persons from the streets into a home where they could die in peace and dignity. She also established an orphanage. Eventually she formed a congregation of sisters, the Missionaries of Charity, whose members are dedicated to serving the extremely poor. The community at present includes about 3,000 sisters of various nationalities who work on five continents. After a lifetime of service to the poor, Mother Theresa died in 1997.

OPRAH WINFREY

Oprah Winfrey was born in 1954 in Kosciusko, Mississippi. A typographical error on her birth certificate produced her name, which was intended to be Orpah. As a child, she lived in Wisconsin and in Tennessee, where she was crowned Miss Black Tennessee at age 19. She attended Tennessee State University, leaving there to become a Nashville television newscaster. She then became a news anchor at an ABC station in Baltimore, which led to a job in Chicago hosting a morning show called *AM Chicago*. The show became number one, was expanded, and was renamed the *Oprah Winfrey Show*.

Winfrey's show is known for exploring people's feelings, and most of her audience seems to adore her. She develops an intimate relationship with her viewers, and readily discloses information about herself that is not easily accessible otherwise.

Oprah owns her own video and film production company, Harpo, Inc. (Oprah spelled backwards). She has also had several acting roles in movies, including *The Color Purple*, *The Women of Brewster Place*, *There Are No Children Here*, and *Beloved*.

ORVILLE WRIGHT

Orville Wright, born in 1871 in Dayton, Ohio, was the son of a clergyman who later became a bishop. Orville and his brother Wilbur demonstrated mechanical abilities at an early age. When they were young boys, their father bought them a toy helicopter, which sparked their interest in flying. Orville built a printing press and started a weekly newspaper while in high school.

In 1892, Orville and his brother opened their own bicycle repair business and soon began making bikes. In 1900, inspired by several glider pioneers, they built their first glider, a biplane, which traveled 300 feet. In 1901 and 1902, they built their second and third gliders.

Orville and Wilbur flew their first powered airplane, *Flyer I,* in 1903 at Kitty Hawk. The flight lasted 12 seconds and covered only 120 feet. In 1904 and 1905, the Wrights built and tested new planes and engines, *Flyer II* and *Flyer III.*

Orville served on the National Advisory Committee for Aeronautics. He died in 1948 in Dayton at the age of seventy-seven.

19. DIVE RIGHT IN!

Purpose

To acknowledge that people react to change in different ways.

Play Time

20 minutes

Physical Activity

None

Participation Format

Unlimited number of teams of 4 to 6

Materials and Preparation

Paper and pencils for each group

Trainer Notes

James Kouzes and Barry Posner talk about a "natural diffusion process" for change in their book, *The Leadership Challenge*. This process, they say, happens over time and involves as many people as possible in its planning and implementation. Kouzes and Posner also state that leaders who link desired organizational changes to employee perceptions and needs are more effective than leaders who impose their personal views.

The goal of this exercise is to help participants understand how differently people react to change, and realize the implications of these differences in handling organizational transitions. Leaders can use their awareness of such differences to plan change efforts that meet employee needs and ways of looking at change.

Directions

1. Divide group into teams of 4 to 6.

2. Ask teams to take 10 minutes to brainstorm as many expressions or sayings as they can think of, related to water or swimming, that deal with reactions to change. For example, "Dive right in" means face change head-on. Answers include but are not limited to:

   - Dive right in
   - Sink or swim
   - Get your feet wet
   - Don't get in too deep
   - Still water runs deep
   - Water over the dam
   - In over our heads
   - We'll have to tread water
   - Like oil and water
   - Make a splash

3. Identify the winning team, which is the team with the most expressions.

4. Instruct people to read some of their expressions and explain how their expressions relate to change.

Debriefing

1. Ask participants:

- What insights have you gained from hearing everyone's responses?

- What implications do these insights have for handling change in your organization?

- Which of the sayings characterizes where your organization is right now? Why?

- Which of the sayings would you like to have as your organization's motto? Why?

2. Summarize by saying that there are many ways to approach change, just as there are many ways to approach water.

How are you entering the water of change (in your organization)? Do you avoid it altogether? Do you have to be dragged in, kicking and screaming? Or do you test it little by little, easing yourself in, thinking that maybe a cool shower would just as easily do the trick? Or do you dive into the surf, attacking the water and taking control of its power?

For some of us, organizational change is cold, scary, and so overwhelming. For others, workplace changes are an exciting adventure, with mysteries and challenges on every crest. There are as many ways to approach business change as there are sandcastle designs and the waves that wash them away.

3. When working with leaders, emphasize the need to recognize the differences in how people react to change and motivate or lead accordingly. For instance, managers should not assume that everyone has the same needs throughout the change process. This means managers need to ask their employees:

- What information do you need?

- What resources do you need?

- What skills do you need?

20. CHANGE MUSCLE BUILDER

Purpose

To focus on skills and resources that help us through change.

Play Time

30 minutes

Physical Activity

None

Participation Format

Unlimited number of groups of 4 to 6

Materials and Preparation

Copy of Change Muscle Builder worksheet for each participant

Trainer Notes

People who successfully make major changes in their lives possess certain identifiable skills, according to Lillie Brock and Mary Ann Salerno in *The InterChange Cycle*™. These skills, or internal resources, include commitment, creativity, focus, responsibility, discipline, courage, and humor.

This exercise emphasizes how important it is for each person to develop and utilize both the skills and resources that contribute to successful change. It helps participants identify the skills and resources they already have and those they can build for themselves or find elsewhere.

Directions

1. Ask participants to take 10 minutes to complete the Change Muscle Builder Worksheet. Indicate that they will be sharing their responses in small groups.

2. Instruct participants to form groups of 4 to 6.

3. Ask participants to share their responses in small groups for the next 10 minutes.

4. Invite a few volunteers to share with the full group.

Debriefing

1. Remind participants that the skills and resources they used in the past may still be available to empower them in the future.

2. Ask the participants the following questions:

   - How many of you found that some of the same skills you use to manage change in your personal lives are those you rely on at work?

   - What are some of the skills you identified?

   - How can you develop the skills you don't yet have?

   - What are some of the resources you listed?

   - What can you do to find or utilize these resources within your organization?

CHANGE MUSCLE BUILDER

1. List some major changes that you've made throughout your life:

_____

_____

_____

_____

_____

_____

_____

2. Why did you make the changes?

_____

_____

_____

_____

_____

3. What skills helped you to make these changes?

_____

_____

_____

_____

_____

4. What resources did you tap?

_____

_____

_____

_____

_____

5. Faced with major changes in the future, would you do anything differently? If so, what?

_____

_____

_____

_____

_____

21. MY HERO! MY HEROINE!

Purpose

To emphasize the skills needed to create or implement change.

Play Time

25 minutes

Physical Activity

None

Participation Format

Pairs

Materials and Preparation

Copy of My Hero! My Heroine! worksheet for each participant

Trainer Notes

In her book, *The Way of the Ronin,* Beverly Potter discusses the skills that are necessary to survive the winds of change at work. Like the displaced samurai of Japan, individuals in today's ever-changing workplaces, according to Potter, must learn critical self-management skills, such as self-motivation, goal setting, self-acknowledgement, avoidance of perfectionism, and incremental commitment.

In this exercise, participants have an opportunity to think about role models in their lives, and to identify which of the role models' admired qualities and skills they already have. The activity also encourages participants to develop those characteristics they do not currently see in themselves.

Directions

1. Ask participants to take 10 minutes to complete the My Hero! My Heroine! worksheet. Explain to participants that a role model is usually someone whose approach to change we admire for some reason. Role models can be friends, parents, brothers or sisters, aunts or uncles, even a famous person we have never met but whose approach to change we admire. Tell participants that they will be sharing their responses.

2. Instruct participants to pair up and to share what they have written with one another.

3. If time allows, ask for examples to be shared with the full group.

Debriefing

1. Ask participants:

   - Who are some of your heroes and heroines? Why did you pick them?

   - How many of you could see yourselves in your role model? (Here the trainer could comment about how we are drawn to others who have qualities we either already have or desire to have.)

   - Which skills of the person you selected will you attempt to demonstrate in your change effort?

2. At the conclusion of the debriefing, acknowledge the wide range of skills mentioned. Explain that the participants may possess some of the same skills as their heroes or heroines. Encourage them to develop those skills that they do not have.

MY HERO! MY HEROINE! WORKSHEET

1. Think of someone in your life whose approach to change you'd like to emulate. List qualities of that person.

   _____   _____   _____

2. How has that person affected your ability to deal with change?

   _____

   _____

   _____

   _____

3. Describe a change you recall that person implementing. What skills did he or she use to accomplish change?

   _____

   _____

   _____

   _____

4. Does your hero or heroine have a favorite bit of advice about facing change? What is it?

   _____

   _____

   _____

   _____

5. Does your hero or heroine remind you of yourself at all? In what ways?

   _____

   _____

   _____

   _____

6. Which skills modeled by your hero or heroine will you demonstrate during your current or next change?

   _____

   _____

   _____

   _____

22. YOU'RE IN CONTROL

Purpose

To acknowledge the level of control and influence we have in creating change.

Play Time

20 minutes

Physical Activity

None

Participation Format

Individual

Materials and Preparation

Copy of You're in Control worksheet for each participant

Trainer Notes

In his book, *Managing at the Speed of Change,* Daryl Conner declares that people become disoriented when they are unable to meet their individual needs for control. Given the amount and speed of change that many people face in their organizations, such disorientation is natural. In fact, during times of great upheaval, it is easy to assume that most people have little control over anything. However, there are always things over which each person has influence, or even authority.

The goal of this exercise is to help participants identify those things over which they have control. It also provides an opportunity for participants to acknowledge those things over which they have no influence or authority, as the first step in letting those things go.

Directions

1. Distribute You're in Control worksheets.

2. Explain the instructions and provide an example.

3. Ask participants to take 10 minutes to answer the questions on the worksheets, and mention that volunteers will be sharing their responses.

Debriefing

1. Invite volunteers to share their responses. Have participants offer tips to each other for ways to take action or let go.

2. Remind participants that when they have control or influence, the most positive behavior is to take action. In fact, they may even need to assertively push for the change. When they do not have control or influence, the most positive action to take is letting go.

YOU'RE IN CONTROL WORKSHEET

List workplace changes that you wish to make, noting those you have control or influence over and those you do not.

Can Control/Influence	Cannot Control/Influence*
_____	_____
_____	_____
_____	_____
_____	_____
_____	_____

What steps can you take to initiate one of the changes you can control or influence?

1. _____

_____

2. _____

_____

3. _____

_____

4. _____

_____

5. _____

_____

*Note: When you cannot control or influence, the most positive action to take is letting go.

23. READY ... AIM!

Purpose

To determine how you can influence another to help you implement a workplace change.

Play Time

20 minutes

Physical Activity

None

Participation Format

Individuals or unlimited number of pairs

Materials and Preparation

Copy of Influencing Others worksheet for each participant

Trainer Notes

The ability to influence others is an essential skill for leading a change process effectively. In *Beyond the Wall of Resistance,* Rick Mauer suggests several ways to exert such influence, including building excitement for changes by actively engaging others, and joining with others and finding common ground to overcome resistance. Mauer says that strategies such as manipulation and "deal-making" are no longer effective in most organizations.

This exercise invites participants to think about an actual situation in which they need to influence someone, and come up with ways they might successfully do so. It emphasizes the importance of planning specific actions that suit each person being influenced.

Directions

1. Ask participants to take 10 minutes, working alone, to complete the Influencing Others worksheet. Inform participants that they will be sharing their responses in pairs at the end of 10 minutes.

2. After participants have had time to answer all the questions, ask participants to talk about their scenarios.

Debriefing

Emphasize the importance of influence in implementing change and how critical it is to plan the influence situation.

INFLUENCING OTHERS TO MAKE THE CHANGE HAPPEN

1. Describe a change that you want to make in the workplace.

   _____

   _____

   _____

   _____

   _____

2. Who do you need to influence to bring about change?

   _____

   _____

   _____

   _____

3. Pick one of the persons listed in question 2 and list 3 reactions that this person will most likely have to your request.

   _____

   _____

   _____

   _____

4. Write a sample scenario showing how you will state your request and how that person will answer.

   _____

   _____

   _____

   _____

   _____

   _____

   _____

   _____

24. HOT BUTTONS

Purpose

To practice responding constructively to people's "hot buttons" as a way of influencing their participation in a change effort.

Play Time

30 minutes

Physical Activity

None

Participation Format

Unlimited number of groups of 4 to 6

Materials and Preparation

Paper and pencils for scribes

Copy and cut Hot Buttons master cards. The master set contains 14 cards.

Trainer Notes

As Daryl R. Conner outlines in *Managing at the Speed of Change*, there are 4 critical roles in the change process: sponsor, agent, advocate, and target. The first 3 roles require strong influencing skills to bring about organizational change efforts.

In this exercise, participants have the opportunity to hone their skills in influencing others by first understanding their target audience's hot buttons—what motivates them. It focuses on how to develop influencing strategies that directly address people's problems, opportunities, hopes, and fears.

Directions

1. Discuss the concept of "hot buttons" with participants as follows:

   Effective influencers analyze their listeners' points of view. Influencers attempt to determine what makes their listeners "tick." In other words, by determining "hot buttons," you are influencing your listeners by addressing their problems, opportunities, hopes, and fears. Also, considering the benefits and disadvantages of what you are proposing from their perspective is helpful in influencing them.

2. Ask participants to form groups of 4 to 6. Distribute 1 card to each group.

3. Direct each group to take 10 minutes to list the "hot buttons" of the audience described on the card it has been assigned. Remind the groups to identify their audience's problems and opportunities, hopes and fears, and benefits or disadvantages of what they are proposing from the audience's perspective. (Fa-

cilitator's note: List these 3 items on a flip chart.) Explain that they will be sharing their lists with the full group and ask them to appoint a scribe for recording answers.

4. At the end of 10 minutes, ask 1 member of each small group to read the audience's description aloud to the full group and then report the potential "hot buttons" that the group identified.

Debriefing

1. At the completion of the discussion, debrief the exercise by asking why the skill of influence is important in implementing organizational change.

2. When working with leaders, remind them that they should be encouraging their teams to consider hot buttons when influencing others. Explain that people don't see the benefit in changing if the change is not something they feel has value to them. When faced with a change, people can't help but ask the question, "What's in it for me?"

This is often seen in the business world. Unless employees are given a sense of the vision—the ultimate goal of the change—and where they fit in, they are going to respond with fear, denial, resistance, stubbornness, anger, resentment, suspicion, ambivalence, or withdrawal. It's critically important that managers faced with change share the vision with employees.

Having a vision—and communicating it—can make the process easier. If someone tells employees why a change has value to them, that might help them accept and, in fact, make the required change.

Adaptations and Variations

You may choose to add situations that are workplace-focused. The authors' experience has shown that people are better able to give attention to what the "hot buttons" might be when people are not actively focused on their current workplace issues. Here are some examples of workplace scenarios you could add:

- Persuading managers to cut their budget to save a business.
- Persuading employees to take on new responsibilities for which they are not yet qualified and will need to be trained.
- Persuading your board of directors to refocus your business according to environmentally sound practices when it is making money as it is.
- Persuading employees to work longer hours to meet an identified customer demand.

HOT BUTTONS CARDS

Persuading a budget committee to invest in new equipment or computer technology.	Persuading members of a professional organization to get more involved in growing and expanding the organization.
Persuading a group of potential investors to provide capital for your business venture.	Persuading a group of concerned citizens to approve an environmental waste incinerator in their community.
Persuading a group of elderly community residents that an increase in school taxes is essential.	Persuading a group of business colleagues to volunteer their time for a community project.
Persuading county commissioners to support the building of an underground tunnel beneath their communities.	Persuading the School Board to require high school students to volunteer 100 hours of public service before graduation.
Persuading the Human Resource department to include a gym membership as a company benefit.	Persuading City Council members to not prohibit the destruction of a 100-year-old landmark.

Persuading the School Board Finance Committee to increase the budget for the arts.	Persuading employees at your corporation to implement a car-pooling system to and from work.
Persuading local corporations and business owners to give money to a philanthropic cause.	Persuading City Council members to destroy an abandoned building and allow for the construction of a playground instead of a new parking garage in the city.

25. CHANGE DEBATE

Purpose

To recognize that there are multiple valid points of view about any change.

Play Time

30 minutes

Physical Activity

None

Participation Format

2 teams of 8 to 10

Materials and Preparation

Prepare a description of an organization change that will occur.

Trainer Notes

Multiple valid points of view are both natural and productive. As American journalist Walter Lippman said, "Where all think alike, no one thinks very much." Dissimilar ideas about change are no exception; they paint a much bigger picture than a single view does.

In this exercise, participants have a chance to speak "for" or "against" an identified organizational change. By inviting a full spectrum of viewpoints, the activity allows participants to express diverse opinions, expand their horizons to include other points, and see a bigger picture.

Directions

1. Divide the group into 2 teams.

2. Present the teams with a change scenario. The change could be, for example, combining departments or moving personnel from one department to another.

3. Designate 1 team "for" the change and 1 team "against" the change.

4. Instruct both teams to take 10 minutes to work up their positions on change in order to present their case. Tell them that they will have 3 minutes to present their positions.

5. At the end of the planning time, ask each team to present a 3-minute overview of its position.

6. Instruct participants to begin a timed debate of 6 minutes, allowing up to 1 minute per comment per team. (This will allow a minimum of 3 comments per team.)

Debriefing

Ask the participants one or more of the following questions:

- What were your feelings about being either "for" or "against" the change?
- What were your feelings about the other team that was opposing you?
- Did you become frustrated during the simulation? If so, why?
- How do you feel about the change situation and being part of it?
- How is the situation similar to what happens in your organizations today?
- What can you draw from this exercise that will help you improve your own organizational change effort?

26. BACK TO THE FUTURE

Purpose

To determine the actions necessary for leaders to create the desired organizational culture.

Play Time

45 minutes

Physical Activity

None

Participation Format

Individuals or an unlimited number of pairs

Materials and Preparation

Copy of Back to the Future worksheet for each participant

Colored felt-tip markers for drawing

Trainer Notes

According to Gary Yukl in *Leadership in Organizations,* a leader's vision of the future is crucial to guiding and coordinating daily decisions during times of change. Clarifying and communicating such a vision provides people with hope for an improved workplace.

This exercise facilitates the development of a vision by giving leaders an opportunity to analyze the current state and future state of their organization. It also helps them identify specific action steps for achieving their organization's desired future.

Directions

1. Direct participants to take 15 minutes to complete the Back to the Future worksheet by drawing a picture or by writing a description of both the current and the desired organizational culture. Additionally, participants should list the actions needed to move from the current to the desired future state.

2. After 15 minutes have elapsed, instruct participants to pair up and to share their worksheet responses with one another. Allow 10 minutes for the pairs to interact.

Debriefing

1. At the end of 10 minutes, debrief the exercise by asking participants to share with the large group 1 statement about their desired organizational culture and 1 action for achieving that outcome.

2. Ask participants:

   - What similarities did you notice in various desired cultures?

   - What about the differences—were there any that were mutually exclusive?

   - What conclusions would you make about defining a vision of the future? (Responses might include: important to agree before you start; people often have different visions; can get into trouble if everyone acts on own vision.)

   - What about the actions? How easy or difficult was it to come up with them?

   - What conclusions can you draw from your experience in defining actions? (Possible responses include: it's easy when you're clear about the future; it's harder than I thought it would be; everyone's actions are different based on their desired future.)

   - How might you apply these conclusions about future visions and necessary actions to your organizational change process?

Adaptations and Variations

When using this exercise with intact workgroups (rather than with groups of leaders), ask each member of the workgroup to share in step 1 of the debriefing. Write the responses on a flip chart as a record of the group's shared vision. This will add time to the exercise.

BACK TO THE FUTURE WORKSHEET

Current State of Organizational Culture

Draw a picture or write a description of the current organizational culture.

Desired Future State of Organizational Culture

Draw a picture or write a description of the desired future state of the organizational culture.

List actions to be taken to move from current state to desired future state.

27. RAINDROPS ON ROSES

Purpose

To increase organizational leaders' awareness of the needs people have as they experience organizational change.

Play Time

30 minutes

Physical Activity

None

Participation Format

Unlimited number of groups of 4 to 6

Materials and Preparation

Copy of Raindrops on Roses worksheet for each participant

Trainer Notes

Employees are an enormous source of power for improving organizational performance, according to John Kotter, author of *Leading Change*. Effectively unleashing this power in alignment with a clear, organizationwide vision involves providing employees with appropriate and needed structures, training, systems, and supervision.

This exercise raises participants' awareness of what people need as they move through a major change. It focuses specifically on the information, skills, and resources required to make a desired change happen.

Directions

1. Instruct participants to form groups of 4 to 6.

2. Ask groups to take 10 minutes to discuss and complete the worksheet.

Debriefing

1. Allow about 10 minutes for volunteers from each group to share their ideas with the entire group.

2. Ask participants:

   • How accessible is each listed item in your organization?

   • What could be done to make other items available for those who need them?

Note to facilitator: Possible responses are found on the Raindrops on Roses Sample Answer Worksheet.

RAINDROPS ON ROSES WORKSHEET

In order for a plant to grow and thrive, certain needs must be met. List them below:

_____
_____
_____
_____
_____
_____
_____
_____
_____
_____
_____
_____
_____

In order for individuals to grow and thrive in a changing environment, certain needs must be met. List them below:

_____
_____
_____
_____
_____
_____
_____
_____
_____
_____
_____
_____
_____

RAINDROPS ON ROSES SAMPLE ANSWER WORKSHEET

In order for a plant to grow and thrive, certain needs must be met. List them below:

- Light
- Water
- Nutrients
- Caretaker

In order for individuals to grow and thrive in a changing environment, certain needs must be met. List them below:

- Information
- Resources
- Skills
- Authority
- Effective Leader

28. OBSTACLE ILLUSION

Purpose

To identify obstacles to organizational change.

Play Time

45+ minutes (for class size of 20)

Physical Activity

Some

Participation Format

Unlimited number of groups of 4 to 6

Materials and Preparation

1 bag per group filled with different items, such as pipe cleaners, straws, construction paper, tape, and paper clips

Trainer Notes

Obstacles are likely to arise no matter how people perceive an announced change. In his book, *Managing at the Speed of Change,* Daryl R. Conner proposes that some resistance to change will occur regardless of whether people see the change as positive or negative. Consequently, the key to any change effort is preparing to overcome resistance, along with other obstacles.

The goal of this exercise is to help participants identify potential obstacles and proposed solutions for implementing organizational changes. It focuses on the specific actions leaders and employees can take to facilitate a successful change.

Directions

1. Instruct participants to form groups of 4 to 6.

2. Ask groups to take 20 minutes to create a product from the contents of the bag that is designed to assist them through the obstacles of organizational change.

3. When 20 minutes have elapsed, ask each group to take 2 to 3 minutes to present its product to the large group.

_____

Note to facilitator: Please note on a flip chart each obstacle to organizational change mentioned.

Debriefing

1. Review the list of obstacles and ask the group for examples of actions they have seen people take in organizations to overcome these obstacles.

2. Ask participants:

   - Which of these actions need to be taken by organizational leaders and managers?

   - Which actions can individual employees take to overcome obstacles associated with organizational change?

29. WRESTLING RESISTANCE

Purpose

To discover leadership strategies for reducing potential resistance to organizational change.

Play Time

30 minutes

Physical Activity

None

Participation Format

Individuals or unlimited number of groups of 4 to 6.

Materials and Preparation

Flip chart and markers or overhead transparency and transparency markers, with question listed in step 1

Copy of Strategies for Leaders: Reducing Potential Resistance to Change handout for each participant

Trainer Notes

Resistance is energy. Instead of trying to reduce resistance, which inevitably reduces available productive energy, it is possible to reroute resistant energy for positive results. Richard Beckhard and Wendy Pritchard, in *Changing the Essence,* advocate addressing the underlying reasons for resistance as the key to propelling energy toward desired changes.

This exercise involves having participants identify possible reasons for resisting change by thinking about their own past resistance to changes. It then solicits strategies for addressing the identified reasons.

Directions

1. Direct participants to take 5 minutes to answer the question, "When I have resisted change in the past, I have done so because …" (Refer participants to the question printed on the overhead transparency or flip chart.)

2. Instruct participants to form groups of 4 to 6 and share their responses. Ask groups to identify strategies that could have reduced the resistance described. Allow participants 15 minutes to complete these tasks.

3. Ask for groups to share their strategies with the large group. Record strategies on a flip chart or overhead transparency.

Debriefing

Summarize the group's comments. Distribute the handout entitled Strategies for Leaders: Reducing Potential Resistance to Change and mention any points on the sheet that participants did not identify.

STRATEGIES FOR LEADERS: REDUCING POTENTIAL RESISTANCE TO CHANGE

1. Provide information early and often to employees.

2. Seek input and involvement of employees.

3. Explain reasons for change.

4. Communicate vision for future.

5. Tell what will change and what will not change.

6. Acknowledge any potential losses.

7. Demonstrate the behavior expected of others.

8. Tell employees "what's in it for them."

9. Don't be afraid to acknowledge the unknown.

10. Don't hesitate to acknowledge fears when appropriate.

11. Provide employees with training or on-the-job coaching.

12. Acknowledge small wins or successes.

30. *THESE* ARE THE GOOD OLD DAYS!

Purpose

To recognize that there is constant, inevitable change in our lives and that we can use what we have learned about past changes to help us through current changes.

Play Time

25 minutes

Physical Activity Level

None

Participation Format

Individual

Materials and Preparation

Slides or overhead transparencies

Slide projector or overhead projector

Screen

Trainer Notes

In his book, *Leading Change,* John Kotter predicts that organizations will experience very fast-paced changes over the next two decades. One way for leaders to prepare for rapid and unknown changes, according to Kotter, is to reflect on how they managed change effectively in the past.

This exercise give participants an opportunity to get ready for future changes by assessing past changes. They might, for example, realize that they need a specific reason to change, or that it is important to acknowledge what is in their control and what is out of their control.

Directions

1. Introduce this exercise by explaining to participants that change is constant and inevitable, as evidenced by the examples they are about to view.

2. Show 10 changes using overhead transparencies or slides, commenting on each. Suggested slides are:

   • Headquarters of their company, past and present

   • A product of their business, past and present

   • First telephone, present telephone

   • Eyeglasses, past and present

- Phonograph, CD player
- First car, latest model
- Hair dryer, past and present
- First airplane, today's jet plane
- Tree with leaves, tree without leaves
- Infant, elderly person

- First iron, today's iron
- First typewriter, personal computer
- Bathing tub, today's whirlpool and tub combination
- First fan (hand-held), modern fan
- Foundation of house, fully built house

3. What conclusions about change can you draw from these slides?

Debriefing

When debriefing, summarize the answers given in step 3 and include any of the following that may not have been identified:

- We have already experienced a great amount of change and we have survived!
- We already know a great deal about handling change, and we can use what we have learned to help us now.
- Each of us is unique in the way we choose to handle changes in our lives.
- We all need a reason, a "why," to go through change.
- We all need to recognize our capacity for controlling the change or for influencing others through it.
- For the most part, changes are either imposed upon us or initiated by us. It's how we manage ourselves through the process that makes a difference.
- We all need to be aware of the different elements of a change and consider our options before acting.
- Some change can be controlled, some can't.
- Everything changes over time.
- Change is most obvious when looking back at the "old" way.
- It helps to know your options when facing change.

Music, Art, and Literature

31. NAME THAT CHANGE

Purpose

To raise awareness of similarities and differences in viewpoints about change.

Play Time

45 minutes

Physical Activity

Some

Participation Format

30 participants or fewer

Materials and Preparation

None

Trainer Notes

Motivating people to change can be challenging, according to Murry M. Dalziel and Stephen C. Schoonover, authors of *Changing Ways*. Change leaders who understand that people have individualized views about change, as well as different styles of coping with change, are better prepared to address individual needs during a change process.

This creative and fun exercise uses song lyrics to demonstrate how different people view change. The goals are to generate an understanding of divergent views and to emphasize how people can learn from each other.

Directions

1. Ask each participant to take 5 minutes to think of a song that describes the way he or she views change. Suggest a few titles to get them started. (For an example, you could use "Sunrise, Sunset.")

2. Instruct the large group to form small groups of 6 and take 15 minutes to share the song titles, a few lines from the song, and why participants chose their songs. Also ask each group to choose 1 song to sing to the full group.

3. After the large group gathers again, ask each group to perform its song.

Debriefing

1. Encourage participants to share what insights they have after hearing these songs. For instance, they might note the similarities or differences in viewpoints.

2. Ask participants:

   - What common themes did you notice?

   - How similar or dissimilar were the songs?

   - How many could identify with more than 1 song?

   - How many of you found that you could not identify at all with some of the songs?

   - In what ways does having many different views about change help or hinder implementing change in an organization?

3. Summarize the discussion by mentioning how exciting and challenging it is that we are so different. We can all learn from one another's perspectives.

32. LESSONS LEARNED

Purpose

To acknowledge the impact our early experiences have had on our approach to change, and to identify how we can modify our future actions based on our past experiences.

Play Time

45 minutes

Physical Activity

None

Participation Format

Unlimited number of groups of 4 to 6

Materials and Preparation

Copy of the Lessons Learned worksheet for each participant

Trainer Notes

In his book, *Transitions,* William Bridges writes that some reactions to change relate more to residual memories of past changes than to a present change. He says that people must acknowledge this influence from past experiences in order to move through a current transition. In addition, Bridges recommends that people look closely at what they learned in the past to inform their present approach to change.

The goal of this exercise is to help participants draw upon what they know about themselves from past changes to find effective ways of responding to change in the present and the future. For example, a person who failed to face a past situation in a healthy way might feel motivated to take more positive actions in similar future situations.

Directions

1. Ask participants to complete the Lessons Learned worksheet. Indicate that they will have 10 minutes to complete this task.

2. Instruct participants to form groups of 4 to 6 people and take 15 minutes to share their experiences, identifying 1 lesson that each person learned.

3. After small groups have finished, ask participants:

   - How many found that your early experience influenced how you deal with change?

   - Who is willing to share an example?

   - What are some of the lessons learned?

- How could these lessons in handling change be used in your organization?

- Who is willing to share 1 thing that you would like to change about your approach to handling change? Why do you want to change your approach?

Debriefing

Ask for thoughts and reactions to the exercise. Possible responses are:

- "I managed to survive."
- "I'm a better person because of the experiences I've had."
- "I had the skills (or resources) needed to handle the change."

LESSONS LEARNED
WORKSHEET

1. In the space below, draw a picture of an event from your past in which you had to deal with change. Examples may include: starting school, participating in a sport, experiencing the death of a pet, meeting your best friend, moving to a new town, or going through the divorce of your parents.

2. Describe your feelings or reactions.

_____

_____

_____

_____

_____

3. How do you think that early event may have affected your ability to deal with change?

_____

_____

_____

_____

_____

4. Describe some typical ways you approach problems or change now.

_____

_____

_____

_____

_____

5. Do you wish you could handle change differently? If so, list 3 ways in which you would like to attempt to approach change from now on.

_____

_____

_____

33. OH, THE PLACES YOU'LL GO

Purpose

To identify reactions and responses to change.

Play Time

30 minutes

Physical Activity

Some

Participation Format

Unlimited number of groups of 4 to 6

Materials and Preparation

Flip chart and markers

Copy of book entitled *Oh, the Places You'll Go!,* by Dr. Seuss (Read through the book in advance. It was published by Random House, 1990.)

Trainer Notes

In their book, *Changing Ways,* Murray M. Dalziel and Stephen C. Schoonover write about six roles that must be filled to implement organizational change: Inventor, Entrepreneur, Integrator, Expert, Manager, and Sponsor. As people perform these roles, their individual perceptions about change influence their own success and the overall success of the change effort.

In this exercise, participants have an opportunity to share their thoughts about a Dr. Seuss book, focusing on the different characters' reactions to change. Afterward, they apply their observations to changes taking place in their organization.

Directions

1. Tell participants that in a few minutes they will be listening to a book entitled *Oh, the Places You'll Go!,* which is geared toward adults and was written by Dr. Seuss. Ask them to listen carefully for the points the story makes about ways we can react or respond to change.

2. Read the story.

3. Divide the large group into small groups of 4 to 6 and ask them to identify the different reactions to change identified in the story. Ask them to discuss how these ideas might apply to personal and organizational change. Ask each group to appoint a scribe to capture the group's ideas on flip chart paper. Allow about 10 minutes for discussion.

Debriefing

1. Ask each group to identify responses to change that are included in *Oh, the Places You'll Go!* Answers might include:

   - We can view the path to change as either difficult or fun.

   - We can experience the road to change as scary or confusing.

   - We can rely on the fact that "this too shall pass."

   - We can act on the assumption that the only way to bring about change is to begin.

   - We are the ones who have responsibility for navigating ourselves through change.

   - We have choices about the way we react to change.

   - A positive attitude about change can help us overcome the obstacles to change.

2. Ask participants:

   - Which of these ideas best fits your organization?

   - Which idea is ideal for your organization in the long run?

Adaptation and Variation

Get 1 copy of the book for each small group and ask them to take turns reading.

34. CHANGE CHOICES

Purpose

To recognize the importance of identifying and selecting options in the change process.

Play Time

30 minutes

Physical Activity

None

Participation Format

Unlimited number of groups of 4 to 6

Materials and Preparation

Paper and pencils

Copy of the poem, "The Road Not Taken," by Robert Frost

Trainer Notes

Failing to recognize the need for updated goals or alternative options can derail the best-planned change effort. Erik Olesen, in *Mastering the Winds of Change*, offers strategies for various points in the change process for assessing how things are going; what new options, if any, are viable; and what new road is visible on the horizon.

This exercise explores how each decision in a change effort requires people to leave something behind or to bypass tempting alternatives. By recognizing the continual need to make choices during organizational transitions, participants can see that a seemingly "big" change is really a series of smaller, manageable choices.

Directions

1. Read the Frost poem aloud to the group, using inflection to emphasize meaning.

2. Ask participants to think about a change they have been through or one they are currently experiencing. Encourage them to identify mutually exclusive choices they have made or must make, or "roads" they have chosen or must choose. Ask participants to record their answers, allowing them 5 minutes to do so.

3. Request that participants form groups of 4 to 6 and share (as they feel comfortable) their changes and choices. Allow 15 minutes.

Debriefing

Gather the large group back together. Ask for volunteers to share their insights about the importance of identifying options as they relate to organizational and personal change. Emphasize that identifying options can help us to move forward and can make change seem less overwhelming.

35. THE POET'S CORNER

Purpose

To provide a creative forum for expressing varying viewpoints on change.

Play Time

45 minutes

Physical Activity

None

Participation Format

Unlimited number of groups of 4 to 6

Materials and Preparation

Paper and pencils or pens

Flip chart and markers or overhead transparency and transparency markers with the instructions listed in step 1

Overhead projector and screen (if using transparency)

Trainer Notes

Each individual's response to change is affected, in part, by his or her type of thinking, according to Ned Herrmann, author of *The Whole Brain Business Book*. Herrmann distinguishes 4 thinking types—logical, organized, expressive, and imaginative—and says that the most creative thinking comes from exercising all 4 types (whole brain thinking). An organization going through changes can develop its "whole brain" by drawing on the differences among its employees.

This creative exercise provides participants with a forum for sharing their differing views about change. It can also help them see how their combined views create a broad perspective of their organization's desired changes.

Directions

1. Explain the following instructions, which you have also written on the flip chart or overhead transparency:

   - Form groups of 4 to 6.

   - Ask each person to offer 1 word he or she associates with change.

   - After the person speaks the word, everyone in the group repeats it 3 times in unison and writes it on his or her list. Allow each person to offer 2 words.

- Create a group poem about change using the list of 8 to 12 words or their derivatives.

2. Ask participants to form small groups and follow the instructions outlined in step 1. Let the participants know they will have 30 minutes to complete their task.

3. After gathering the large group back together, ask each group to read its creation. (Ask for 6 volunteers if the group size is over 30.)

Debriefing

Ask participants to comment on the various viewpoints that emerged about change. Emphasize that finding creative outlets for expressing our reactions to change is healthy and allows us to deal with change more positively.

36. INSPIRATION INFORMATION

Purpose

To gain insight into what inspires people in times of transition.

Play Time

35 minutes

Physical Activity

None

Participation Format

Unlimited number of groups of 4 to 6

Materials and Preparation

Instructor's selection of a poem or quote

Participants' selected poems or quotes (Instruct participants ahead of time to bring a copy of a poem or quote that has been helpful to them in times of transition.)

Extra copies of poems or quotes for participants who need them

Trainer Notes

All change elicits some degree of resistance in most people. In his book, *Beyond the Wall of Resistance,* Rick Mauer says that while exploring resistance is both difficult and dangerous, such exploration is necessary if leaders are to manage change efforts effectively. In fact, understanding their own resistance and keeping themselves motivated during times of transition are 2 essential factors in leaders' success in bringing about real change.

This exercise encourages participants to identify resources that have motivated them during times of change. It emphasizes how important it is for people to keep themselves inspired in the midst of change.

Directions

1. Check to see that each group member has an inspirational poem or quote.

2. Read your poem or quote and explain why you find this resource helpful in transitional periods.

3. Divide the large group into small groups of 4 to 6 and instruct them to take 20 minutes to share poems and quotes.

4. After small group sharing, ask for a few volunteers to share with the large group.

Debriefing

Emphasize the importance of surrounding ourselves with inspirational resources in times of transition. Ask participants about other ways they or other people can keep themselves inspired in the midst of change at work. Record responses on the flip chart. Emphasize that inspirational thoughts can positively influence our own self-talk.

37. CINEMATIC CHANGES

Purpose

To reinforce the need for resources and skills when creating and managing change.

Play Time

20 minutes

Physical Activity

None

Participation Format

Individuals

Materials and Preparation

Flip chart and markers or overhead transparency and transparency markers

Overhead projector and screen (if using transparency)

Trainer Notes

In her book, *The Power of Partnering: Vision, Commitment, and Action,* Joanne G. Sujansky explains that no matter how change starts, its success depends on quickly and accurately assessing certain needs. Whether the change comes from seizing an unexpected opportunity or solving a long-standing problem, making it happen depends on identifying the necessary information, skills, and resources, and then following through to supply them.

This exercise asks participants to think of movies in which major changes have been depicted, and then identify the resources used by the main character to deal with the change. Participants then determine the usefulness of the film's basic message to their organization today.

Directions

1. Ask the group to think of movies that depict change of any kind—personal, political, or societal.

2. Begin the exercise by suggesting 2 or 3 titles, for example, *The Wizard of Oz, A Christmas Carol,* or *Big.*

3. List movie names on the flip chart or overhead transparency. For each movie listed, ask participants to identify what resources or skills the main character relied on for managing change. Also ask for the film's underlying message. Record participants' responses.

Debriefing

Solicit reactions to the movies selected and the comments made about them. Additionally, ask participants:

- Which resources and skills on the list are available in your organization?
- Which ones could you develop?
- Which of the messages is most helpful for your organization at this point in time?

Emphasize the need for each of us to identify resources necessary for managing ourselves through the changes in our lives.

Adaptations and Variations

You may choose to ask participants to distinguish between resources and skills that are internal (within individuals) and those that are external. Individuals could determine what internal skills and resources they have and could develop. Groups could determine what external skills and resources they have and could develop.

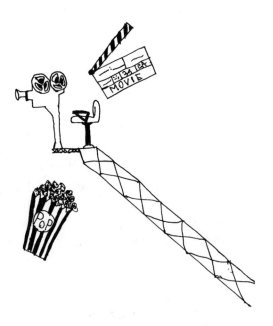

38. SINGING ... FOR A CHANGE

Purpose

To acknowledge the inevitability of organizational change and the impact it has on employees.

Play Time

45 minutes

Physical Activity

Some

Participation Format

Unlimited number of groups of 4 to 6

Materials and Preparation

None

Trainer Notes

As Douglas K. Smith notes in *Taking Charge of Change*, there are many forces of change, such as technology, demographics, government policy, and financial markets. While change is inevitable, its effects on people can vary.

In this exercise, participants have a chance to describe the effects of organizational change on employees. The lighthearted activity highlights the common elements in people's experience of change.

Directions

1. Divide the large group into smaller groups of 4 to 6.

2. Ask the groups to write new lyrics to a familiar tune, such as "Row, Row, Row Your Boat" or "I've Been Working on the Railroad." The lyrics should describe the changes going on in their workplace(s) and the impact on the employees.

3. Allow participants 30 minutes for writing and practicing their songs.

4. Ask each group to entertain the full group with its song. When there are only 3 or 4 small groups, ask the groups to sing songs consecutively. Otherwise, intersperse the songs throughout the workshop day(s).

Debriefing

Solicit reactions to the songs, especially to the lyrics. Comment on any patterns you notice regarding types of changes mentioned in the lyrics and the impacts on people.

Adaptation and Variation

Participants may want to have their songs collected into a songbook so that each of them may have one as a reminder of the experience. You may wish to solicit a volunteer to make the songbooks.

39. A JOURNEY INTO THE FUTURE: A GUIDED IMAGERY EXERCISE

Purpose

To help participants experience potential outcomes for a change with which they are dealing.

Play Time

60 minutes

Physical Activity

None

Participation Format

Individuals or groups of 4 to 6

Materials and Preparation

Plain paper

CD or tape player and instrumental, soft music

Colored felt-tip markers for drawing

Trainer Notes

One key to the success of organizational change is envisioning the outcomes of desired changes. Burt Nanus begins his book, *Visionary Leadership,* by proclaiming, "There is no more powerful engine driving an organization toward excellence and long-range success than an attractive, worthwhile, and achievable vision of the future, widely shared."

This exercise provides participants with an opportunity to define and imagine experiencing their desired outcomes for an identified change. While participants may use the imagery to guide them through personal changes, they can easily translate the experience of defining outcomes to organizational change.

Directions

1. Tell participants that you are going to take them on an imaginary tour or journey that will allow them to explore the possible outcomes related to an upcoming change. Explain that in a few minutes you will be asking them to get comfortable and close their eyes, if they choose. You will be playing soft music and will guide them as they travel to the future to discover what possibilities appear for them about an upcoming change. Remind them that whatever appears is okay (including a blank screen).

2. Use or adapt following script to meet your needs and style: (Dim the lights and put on soft music before you begin.)

- Please get comfortable, with your feet flat on the floor and outstretched palms on your lap. Close your eyes, if you are comfortable doing so.

- Release the tension in your head, neck, shoulders, chest, abdomen, thighs, calves, and legs, finally sending any remaining tension out through your toes.

- Imagine yourself in a place of beauty, a place that has special meaning for you, a place of safety, a place of calm and serenity.

- What does that place:
  - look like?
  - smell like?
  - sound like?
  - taste like?
  - What textures do you feel?

- Take a few minutes to enjoy yourself in your special place.

- Think about a change that you are facing.

- What excites you about this change?

- What concerns you about this change?

- See yourself handling that change in a positive manner. Let time pass, then imagine that everything about this change turned out positive. Look around; what do you:
  - see?
  - smell?
  - taste?
  - touch?
  - hear?

- What are you feeling? What are you thinking?

- When in the future are you? What year and month is it?

- Now see yourself moving closer back to your special place and finally back to today.

- Thank yourself for taking the journey and slowly, when you are ready, open your eyes and return in your mind to this room.

3. Ask participants to take 20 minutes to draw (or write about) what came to their minds. Indicate that they will be sharing in small groups later.

4. After 20 minutes have elapsed, instruct participants to form groups of 4 to 6.

5. Instruct small groups to take a total of 15 minutes to share the highlights of their journeys with one another.

Debriefing

Ask participants to describe the value to them of this exercise, and record their responses on a flip chart. Responses might include:

- Focused on outcome(s) for which you need to take responsibility.
- Focused on positive aspects of change.
- Used the right brain in examining change.
- Looked at a change from a holistic approach.
- Considered skills and resources necessary for managing change.
- Focused on where we are going, which makes the future seem less scary.

Comment that these same ideas apply to looking at full-scale organizational change.

40. A TALE OF THE WATER OF LIFE

Purpose

To identify the importance of using all available resources in times of crisis and change.

Play Time

15 minutes

Physical Activity

None

Participation Format

Individual

Materials and Debriefing

Practice reading the story a few times. You might even consider memorizing it.

Trainer Notes

In *Discontinuous Change*, authors David Nadler, Robert Shaw, and A. Elise Walton assert that major transitions involve fairly large risks for an organization. Consequently, change efforts require significant resources, such as people, training, money, and consulting support, to reduce risks and achieve desired results.

This exercise helps participants understand the importance of using all available resources in times of crisis and transition. It does so by focusing on what can help or hinder the success of a major organizational change.

Directions

Tell participants that you are going to share a portion of a Grimm's fairy tale and you would like them to be thinking about how it might relate to change. The story goes as follows:

> *This is a story about a sick king, his three sons, a little man, and the water of life.*
>
> *There once was a king who was desperately ill. His sons went to the garden to weep and met an old man who told them about the water of life, which was difficult to find but could restore their father to health.*
>
> *They told their father about this water, but the king feared the danger would be too great in finding it and begged his sons not to go. The oldest son, however, thought to himself that if he found this water, he would inherit the kingdom, and so he set off to find the water.*
>
> *As he traveled, he met a little man who asked him, "Where are you going so quickly?" The oldest son asked, "Why should I tell you?" With that the little man wished an evil*

thing, and the oldest brother rode into a narrow mountain pass that became so narrow that he got stuck.

When the oldest brother did not return, the second brother (in hopes of inheriting the kingdom) set off to find the water of life. Again the little man appeared and asked, "Where are you going?" to which the second son replied, "Why do you want to know?" For the second time the little man wished something evil, and the second brother came to the same narrow pass as his older brother and got stuck—unable to move forward, backward, or sideways.

When the second brother did not return, the youngest brother set out to find the water that would cure his father. He too met the little man, who asked him, "Where are you going?" The youngest brother replied, "I am seeking the water of life for my father." The little man asked, "Do you know where to find it?" The youngest son replied, "No." The little man then offered to help the youngest brother find it, because "he had behaved as he ought."

The story goes on to tell how the little man helped the youngest son with this impossible task.

Debriefing

Ask the participants how this story might be related to what facilitates and what hinders organizational change. Possible answers might include:

Facilitates

- Working as a team to overcome obstacles.
- Using all possible resources in times of change or crisis.
- Being open to receiving help.
- Not trying to do it alone.

Hinders

- Being self-serving.
- Not letting others help you.
- Not communicating with others—not letting them know what you're doing.

41. COLLAGE CREATION

Purpose

To identify strategies that leaders use to create and implement change.

Play Time

60 minutes

Physical Activity

Some

Participation Format

Unlimited number of groups of 4 to 6

Materials and Preparation

Flip chart and markers

Distribute the following materials throughout the room just prior to the exercise:

Variety of magazines (5 or 6 per table)

Scissors (2 or 3 per table)

Glue (2 bottles or sticks per table)

Markers and poster board (1 of each per group)

Trainer Notes

In his book, *Leading Change,* John Kotter proposes that the biggest mistake leaders can make when trying to change their organizations is to forge ahead without cultivating a sense of urgency in the people responsible for making the change happen. Other important leadership skills, according to Kotter, include the ability to communicate effectively, to share a clear vision, and to anticipate problems.

In this exercise, participants define a set of skills beneficial to leaders of change. In addition, they determine which skills are already in evidence within their organization and which skills need to be developed.

Directions

1. Divide the large group into groups of 4 to 6.

2. Call attention to the location of the materials. Instruct participants to cut pictures from the magazines or draw pictures to make a team collage that defines the skills needed for leading change. Tell them that they have 30 minutes to complete this task.

3. Ask groups to display and describe their collages. As skills are shared, record them on the flip chart.

Debriefing

1. Reinforce the key leadership skills mentioned by the small groups. Ask participants:

   - Which of these skills are being used in your organization now?

   - Which of these skills can be developed more?

2. Comment that during a change effort, leaders are encouraged to:

   - Communicate early, thoroughly, frankly, and often.

   - Listen as much as (or more than) they speak.

   - Set an example of resilience, acceptance, and positive thinking.

   - Help others see the value in changing—share the vision.

   - Let employees be a part of the change process, the decision making, and the goal setting.

   - Recognize that all people handle change differently.

Adaptation and Variation

Use this activity for nonleader groups by asking participants to create a team collage that defines the skills needed for self-managing change.

Closure
Activities

42. HOW 'BOUT THIS?

Purpose

To reinforce the need for action and positive thinking when taking personal responsibility for change.

Play Time

50 minutes

Physical Activity Level

None

Participation Format

Unlimited number of groups of 4 to 6

Materials and Preparation

Copy of Plan for Change worksheet for each participant

Felt-tip markers for drawing

Trainer Notes

J.W. Goethe said, "Whatever you can do, or dream you can, begin it. Boldness has genius, power, and magic in it." In this quote, he is inviting people to take personal responsibility for themselves and their lives. His advice is relevant today to organizations going through major change.

This exercise gives participants a chance to take personal responsibility for how a desired change will occur in their organization. It directs each individual to focus on a specific change, identify "what's in it for me," and envision the best possible results.

Directions

1. Ask participants to take up to 15 minutes to complete the Plan for Change worksheets.

2. Instruct participants to form groups of 4 to 6 to share their worksheet responses (1 participant at time), and then take turns suggesting possible action steps for each participant's Plan for Change, starting their sentences with "How

'bout this ..." Allow 10 or 15 minutes so that all participants have a turn receiving suggestions.

3. Instruct the person who is receiving the suggestions to respond positively, for example, saying "Thank you, I'll try that," or "Tell me more about that," or "Sounds like a great idea."

Debriefing

Ask participants:

- What are the benefits of identifying actions steps when implementing change?
- What are the benefits of asking for or getting help from others?
- What are the benefits of imagining a positive result?

PLAN FOR CHANGE WORKSHEET

1. Describe a work-related change you are thinking of making. List the reasons you would like to make the change. Is it for an emotional reason, such as lessening stress? Is it to help your family or a friend? Is it for health or money reasons, or simply for fun?

_____

_____

_____

_____

_____

2. Now, list the pros and cons of making the change. What might you gain? What might you lose?

Pros/Gains	Cons/Losses
_____	_____
_____	_____
_____	_____
_____	_____
_____	_____

3. Imagine the pros/gains have occured. Draw a picture of that on the reverse side.

43. IF YOU COULD SEE ME NOW!

Purpose

To reaffirm the importance of identifying actions that support a future vision.

Play Time

25 minutes

Physical Activity Level

None

Participation Format

Unlimited number of pairs

Materials and Preparation

Paper and pencils

Your prepared answer to step 1

Trainer Notes

Jon R. Katzenbach and the RCL Team, in *Real Change Leaders*, write about the benefits of developing "working visions"—desired outcomes that are both practical and positive. From working visions come realistic actions that ultimately produce the original vision.

In this exercise, participants look ahead 1 year and focus on outcomes that occurred from actions they took during the last 12 months. It emphasizes the importance of having a vision and acknowledging the progress made toward that vision.

Directions

1. Ask participants to imagine that it is 1 year from now. Direct them to take 5 minutes to write a paragraph about the past year based on actions that they have already taken to create necessary changes. (Before participants begin their work, share your answer.)

2. Have each participant share his or her paragraph with 1 other person, allowing 2 to 3 minutes per person to do so.

3. Invite 2 or 3 volunteers to share their paragraphs with the whole group.

Debriefing

Emphasize to the group that we become what we diligently set out to become. The vision of what we want to become can be a motivating factor for change.

44. HABIT-BREAKING ENDING

Purpose

To reinforce the importance of committing to productive behaviors when implementing change.

Play Time

30 minutes

Physical Activity Level

None

Participation Format

Unlimited number of groups of 4 to 6

Materials and Preparation

Copy of Ø sign for each participant

Trainer Notes

When Mark Twain wrote that "A habit cannot be tossed out the window, it must be coaxed down the stairs a step at a time," he was suggesting that it takes a while to break a habit. His advice applies to today's organizational transitions: It is possible for people to coax out habits that interfere with their ability to cope with organizational changes, and replace those habits with more productive behaviors.

This exercise helps participants identify and get rid of 1 or more personal habits that hamper their efforts to implement change at work. It also helps them identify replacement behaviors, while acknowledging that changing their behavior can take time.

Directions

1. Distribute a Ø sign to each participant.

2. Ask each person to take 5 minutes to think of 1 personal behavior that has hampered his or her ability to implement change at work, such as procrastination or worry.

3. Instruct participants to use a marker to write the behavior on the Ø sign, and indicate below the sign the replacement behavior. (Show your own sign as an example.) Tell them that they will be sharing their completed signs in small groups.

4. Divide the large group into groups of 4 to 6 and ask participants to take 1 minute each to show and tell about their signs.

Debriefing

1. Mention the importance of identifying unproductive behaviors and replacing them with positive ones. (Use your own example to make this point.)

2. Encourage participants to hang their signs in a visible place so that they are reminded each day of their commitment to quit the unproductive behavior and begin the productive behavior.

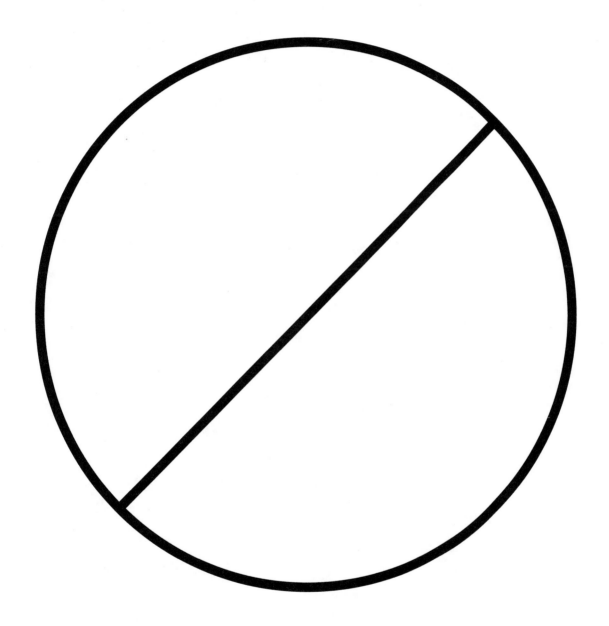

45. THE ARTSY ENDING

Purpose

To express creatively or dramatically what we have learned about the skills and resources needed to implement change.

Play Time

45 minutes

Physical Activity Level

Moderate

Participation Format

30 participants or fewer

Materials and Preparation

Toy musical instruments, hats, pieces of old various costumes, poster board

(Note: It is possible to do this activity with only those items available in the training room area.)

Trainer Notes

The Pursuit of WOW! by Tom Peters is packed with hundreds of statements about skills, attitudes, resources, and behaviors that can help people achieve success in an organizational change effort. They range from "Beware of middle-ground compromises" and "Don't treat change with kid gloves" to "Realize change is as normal as breathing" and "Perception is everything."

In this exercise, participants have an opportunity to summarize what they have learned about the skills and resources that are necessary to implement change successfully within their organization. The activity invites participants to be creative and dramatic.

Directions

1. Divide the group into teams of 4 to 6.
2. Ask each team to create a 1- to 3-minute skit, poem, or song to present to the large group, emphasizing the skills and resources needed to implement change.
3. Allow 20 minutes for writing of skits, poems, or songs.
4. Invite teams to give their presentations to the whole group.

Debriefing

Summarize the skills and resources that were highlighted in the presentations. Emphasize the need for each of us to identify the resources necessary for managing ourselves through the changes in our lives.

46. BUDDY SYSTEM FOLLOW-UP

Purpose

To support participants in taking action following the workshop.

Play Time

30 minutes

Physical Activity Level

None

Participation Format

Unlimited number of pairs

Materials and Preparation

Paper and pencil for each participant

Trainer Notes

Most authors who write about change have prescriptive advice for readers. For example, Erik Olesen, author of *Mastering the Winds of Change,* encourages his readers by saying, "Each of us is a potential peak performer ... capable of being cool, calm, and collected when pressure-packed change occurs." In the final analysis, however, change occurs because of the commitment of each individual within the organization to implement the change.

This exercise gives participants a chance to focus on their commitment to organizational change. During the activity, they list several actions they will take to bring about actual changes in the workplace.

Directions

1. Direct participants to take 10 minutes to write 1 to 2 work-related changes and actions steps that they will take toward each of those changes.

2. Ask them to share their plans with 1 other participant, taking 5 minutes per person. Instruct participants to agree upon a date and a way to contact each other 30 to 60 days following the workshop to check each other's progress.

3. Invite 1 or 2 pairs to summarize their discussion.

Debriefing

Remind participants of the value of action planning and enlisting support from others to successfully implement changes.

47. DEAR ME

Purpose

To reinforce learning and to provide a reminder about the importance of making personal commitments to change.

Play Time

25 minutes

Physical Activity Level

None

Participation Format

Individual

Materials and Preparation

$8\frac{1}{2} \times 11$-inch paper and business-size envelope for each person

Pens

Flip chart or transparency with instructions listed in step 1

Overhead projector and screen (if using transparency)

(Note: Ask the sponsoring organization to provide postage or be prepared to provide it yourself.)

Trainer Notes

In his book, *Managing at the Speed of Change,* Daryl Conner postulates that the lack of full commitment to change contributes to the failure of change efforts. He says that because building commitment to change is often difficult, people should be expressly intentional about making a commitment to change.

This exercise provides participants with a chance to define the specific steps they are willing to take in carrying out their intended workplace changes. It emphasizes the importance of making an individual commitment to common outcomes.

Directions

1. Distribute paper and envelopes.
2. Ask each participant to take 15 minutes to write himself or herself a letter listing the following 3 points (the 3 items should be displayed on a flip chart or overhead transparency):

- The most important learning point from this course.

- Specific action steps (related to workplace change) to be taken during the next 3 months as a result of this training.

- The overall desired outcome.

3. Ask participants to place their letters in the envelopes and address the envelopes to themselves.

4. Tell participants that in about 3 months, they will receive their letters in the mail to remind them of their commitments to change.

Debriefing

1. Emphasize the power of written commitment during the change process.

2. Send the letters to the workshop participants 3 months after the end of the workshop.

48. PACKING A NEW BAG

Purpose

To help participants prepare for a change they choose to make.

Play Time

30 minutes

Physical Activity Level

None

Participation Format

Unlimited number of pairs

Materials and Preparation

One copy of the backpack illustration per participant

Colored felt-tip markers

Trainer Notes

Problems with organizational structure, systems, skills, or supervisors can derail an envisioned change, according to John Kotter, author of *Leading Change*. Removing potential problems involves addressing the needs related to each area and supplying essential resources for keeping the area problem-free. Some of Kotter's suggested needs and resources are: training; new structures that fit the vision; personnel systems that fit the vision; and open systems of communication.

In this exercise, participants direct their attention to the things they'll need to make a desired change over the next 12 months, including tangible and intangible items. They then have a chance to share some of their ideas and talk about how they can obtain the resources they need.

Directions

1. Ask participants to take a few minutes to think about a work-related change they want to make over the next year. Remind them that achieving their goal might take them to a new destination—somewhere they've never been before.

2. Direct participants to focus on what they will need for their "journeys"—both tangible and intangible things. (For example, they might need a resource book and courage.) Allow 3 minutes for this step.

3. Distribute the backpack illustrations and instruct participants to take 5 minutes to write or draw on the backpack outline what they will need for their journeys. Let them know that they may use symbols for the intangible items.

4. Ask participants to choose a partner and take 5 minutes per person to talk about at least 2 items from their backpacks, the reason(s) those items are important to them, and how they can secure the resources.

Debriefing

Emphasize the importance of identifying and marshaling the resources needed for implementing change.

PACKING A NEW BAG

49. "YOU DONE GOOD!" REWARD

Purpose

To reinforce the concept of giving and accepting rewards and recognition for progress made toward a desired change (goal).

Play Time

20 minutes

Physical Activity Level

None

Participation Format

Unlimited number of pairs

Materials and Preparation

Index cards (1 per participant)

Pens and pencils

Trainer Notes

William Bridges, in *Managing Transitions*, emphasizes the importance of reinforcing new beginnings during a change effort. According to Bridges, doing so allows an organization to "keep its new shape." One of the ways organizations can help reinforce a new shape is by rewarding and celebrating small wins and milestones along the way—for individuals and for the organization as a whole.

The goal of this exercise is to help participants identify a reward for themselves that is associated with taking a specific first step toward a desired change. It focuses on taking 1 step at a time and acknowledging each step taken.

Directions

1. Distribute index cards.

2. Ask participants to take 5 minutes to list on their cards the first step they will take in the next 30 days to implement a desired workplace change. Also instruct participants to list a reward for themselves for completing or accomplishing the first step.

3. Direct participants to sign and date the cards and place them where they will see them daily, for example, in their day planners or on their mirrors or nightstands.

4. Ask them to take 10 minutes (5 minutes per person) to share with a partner what they have written.

Debriefing

Ask for examples of first steps and rewards. Additionally, ask participants why identifying first steps as well as rewards is critical to the change process. Possible responses include:

- Helps me keep my eye on the prize (instead of the problem or change).
- Taking the first step gets me started.
- Planning the action step and reward makes the change more real to me.

50. LETTING GO FOR GETTING ON

Purpose

To identify what we must let go of in order to make a desired change.

Play Time

15 minutes

Physical Activity Level

None

Participation Format

Individual

Materials and Preparation

Slips of paper (1 per participant)

One paper or plastic bag

Trainer Notes

The French poet Paul Valery said, "Every beginning is a consequence. Every beginning ends something." In his book, *Managing Transitions,* William Bridges reinforces Valery's thoughts, recommending that in order to begin something new, people must end what used to be.

This exercise facilitates participants' identification of what they need to let go of in order to make a specific organizational change. In addition, it helps them symbolically let go of whatever they identify.

Directions

1. Ask participants to think about a work-related change they want or need to make over the next 3 months.

2. Direct participants to identify 1 thing they will need to let go of or say good-bye to in order to make the change, and to write that item on a slip of paper. (These items can be tangible or intangible.) Examples: "Say good-bye to colleagues" or "Let go of the fear of the unknown."

3. Collect the slips of paper in the small bag. Ceremoniously place it in the garbage bin or offer to take it home and burn it.

Debriefing

- Mention to participants that this is the first step in the ritual of letting go.
- Remind them that because letting go is an ongoing process, they might consider repeating the ceremony at home or at work to reinforce it.

Activities for Breaks and Fillers

WORD SCRAMBLE GAMES

Purpose

To raise awareness of different reactions to change or to the inevitability of change.

Play Time

15 minutes

Physical Activity

None

Participation Format

Individual

Materials and Preparation

Copy of any Word Scramble sheet for each participant

Directions

1. Before a break, announce that a Word Game will be placed at each person's seat and that participants may start the game as soon as the break is over. Tell participants that those who are punctual will have a competitive advantage.

2. Distribute sheets near the end of the break.

3. When the break is over, instruct participants to complete the Word Game. Announce that 1 or more winners will be determined, based on the highest number of correct answers completed within 10 minutes.

4. Let participants know when their playing time has elapsed.

5. Review answers with the group by asking for volunteers to provide them. Ask each person to keep track of his or her correct answers.

6. Identify and acknowledge those with the highest number of correct answers. Award prizes if you choose.

Debriefing

Discuss with participants their reactions to the words in the exercise and their insights about change.

CHANGE WORD SCRAMBLE 1

Unscramble the following words, which are related to change or represent things that change.

1. lisereiecn
2. tinortansi
3. sisatempmorho
4. gheacn
5. ssanoes
6. heassp
7. segats
8. segapssa
9. meeaolchn
10. graholom
11. rtise
12. ttkiy ttrlie
13. ahriod

CHANGE WORD SCRAMBLE 1
ANSWER KEY

1. resilience
2. transition
3. metamorphosis
4. change
5. seasons
6. phases
7. stages
8. passages
9. chameleon
10. hologram
11. tires
12. kitty litter
13. hairdo

CHANGE WORD SCRAMBLE 2 | PARTICIPANT MATERIAL

Unscramble the following words, which are related to change or represent things that change.

1. derwraenu

2. nshfaio

3. desti

4. hawetre

5. zli ylortas' subanhsd

6. smpris

7. doom

8. modo gnris

9. soopkacdiele

10. ylsil upytt

11. sag crieps

12. rainile fraes

CHANGE WORD SCRAMBLE 2 ANSWER KEY

1. underwear
2. fashion
3. tides
4. weather
5. Liz Taylor's husbands
6. prisms
7. mood
8. mood rings
9. kaleidoscope
10. Silly Putty
11. gas prices
12. airline fares

NO CHANGE WORD SCRAMBLE

Unscramble the following words, which describe things that do not change.

1. tangatsn

2. easm

3. ngorbi

4. otriune

5. dialpc

6. odrote

7. tidsa

8. ctuks

9. ibmlemoi

10. aded

NO CHANGE WORD
SCRAMBLE ANSWER KEY

1. stagnant
2. same
3. boring
4. routine
5. placid
6. rooted
7. staid
8. stuck
9. immobile
10. dead

DELAY MOVEMENT WORD SCRAMBLE

Unscramble the following words, which are related to actions that people take to impede change.

1. cirabdera

2. nfoncie

3. otps

4. bnteom

5. spmirion

6. tersrnia

7. senrahs

8. dolh

9. eepidm

10. laht

11. cneleso

DELAY MOVEMENT WORD SCRAMBLE ANSWER KEY

1. barricade
2. confine
3. stop
4. entomb
5. imprison
6. restrain
7. harness
8. hold
9. impede
10. halt
11. enclose

THINGS THAT CHANGE WORD SCRAMBLE

Unscramble the following words, which are related to change or which represent things that change.

1. idwn

2. tlarcelrapi

3. hncolemae

4. atdlepo

5. geg

6. gae

7. wbairno

8. eawreth

9. eplepo

10. gfneiels

11. srepilahtsnio

12. etmi

13. kcocl

14. ealdutti

15. eldoungti

16. edalutit

17. sedeger

THINGS THAT CHANGE WORD SCRAMBLE ANSWER KEY

1. wind
2. caterpillar
3. chameleon
4. tadpole
5. egg
6. age
7. rainbow
8. weather
9. people
10. feelings
11. relationships
12. time
13. clock
14. altitude
15. longitude
16. latitude
17. degrees

CHANGE HAPPENS WORD SCRAMBLE

Unscramble the following words, which are related to change or which represent things that change.

1. oblod surespre
2. arewt vlele
3. nsopmirsesi
4. siiononp
5. tateditsu
6. edncitsa
7. saosesn
8. svelae
9. sfinaho
10. yltsse
11. getwih
12. eerpsurs
13. odmos
14. imteonos
15. pmtreteaeur

CHANGE HAPPENS WORD SCRAMBLE ANSWER KEY

1. blood pressure
2. water level
3. impressions
4. opinions
5. attitudes
6. distance
7. seasons
8. leaves
9. fashion
10. styles
11. weight
12. pressure
13. moods
14. emotions
15. temperature

FIND-A-WORD GAMES

Purpose

To raise awareness of the importance of planning for change.

Play Time

15 minutes

Physical Activity

None

Participation Format

Individual

Materials and Preparation

Copy of Find-a-Word sheets for each participant

Pencils

Overhead transparency of Find-a-Word Answer Key

Directions

1. Before a break, announce that a Word Game will be placed at each person's seat and that participants may start the game as soon as the break is over. Tell participants that those who are punctual will have a competitive edge.

2. Distribute sheets near the end of the break.

3. When the break is over, instruct participants to complete the Word Game. Announce that 1 or more winners will be determined, based on the highest number of correct answers completed within 10 minutes.

4. Let participants know when their playing time has elapsed.

5. Review answers with the group by asking for volunteers to provide them. Refer to the overhead transparency sheet. (You may do this immediately following the exercise or later in the day.) Ask each person to keep track of his or her correct answers.

6. Identify and acknowledge those with the highest number of correct answers. Award prizes if you choose.

Debriefing

Discuss with participants their reactions to the words in the exercise, especially as the words relate to the title of the Find-a-Word Game, and their insights about change.

THINKING ABOUT CHANGE
FIND-A-WORD

In the puzzle, search for and circle the words listed below. Words can be found reading up, down, sideways, backward, and diagonally.

R	E	V	U	P	M	A	P	S	T
E	E	I	A	T	C	A	U	S	E
C	O	S	T	T	S	A	F	A	L
O	A	I	I	S	O	S	F	W	L
M	G	O	F	L	A	M	E	N	T
M	N	N	O	Y	I	Y	F	E	H
E	E	O	N	A	A	E	A	W	E
N	H	N	L	D	E	O	N	E	M
D	W	H	Y	O	D	P	I	C	K
N	A	P	A	T	I	E	N	C	E

SOS	LAMENT	PATIENCE	NAP	GO
AWE	RESILENCE	FAST	ONE	PUFF
DO	IF ONLY	FLAME	IDEA	NEW
ACT	RECOMMEND	TODAY	VISION	WE
PICK	TELL THEM	ASAP	WAS	FYI
COST	ACTION	WHY	REV UP	WHEN
MAPS	CAUSE	NO NO	PASS	

THINKING ABOUT CHANGE
FIND-A-WORD ANSWER KEY

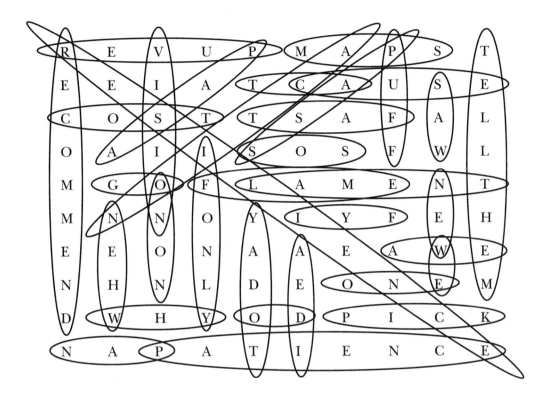

MAKING CHANGE HAPPEN
FIND-A-WORD

In the puzzle, find and circle the words listed below. Words can be found reading up, down, sideways, backward, and diagonally.

```
T   R   A   N   S   F   O   R   M   C
P   E   R   M   T   A   N   E   P   O
O   L   R   R   A   B   J   F   G   M
L   E   I   O   R   T   S   O   O   B
E   A   V   F   T   C   D   E   I   I
V   S   E   N   V   I   S   I   O   N
E   E   N   E   R   G   I   Z   E   E
D   E   L   V   E   R   N   E   C   C
E   X   C   E   L   E   C   R   O   N
T   H   I   E   H   T   R   O   N   E
A   J   A   K   T   S   E   L   N   M
E   P   C   L   R   L   A   P   E   M
R   M   T   N   I   O   S   X   C   O
C   O   A   X   B   B   E   E   T   C
```

ACT	COAX	DELVE	EXPLORE	OPEN
ARRIVE	COMBINE	DEVELOP	FORM	RELEASE
BIRTH	COMMENCE	ENERGIZE	INCREASE	START
BOLSTER	CONNECT	ENVISION	JOIN	TRANSFORM
BOOST	CREATE	EXCEL	LEAP	

MAKING CHANGE HAPPEN
FIND-A-WORD ANSWER KEY

```
T  R  A  N  S  F  O  R  M  C
P  E  R  M  T  A  N  E  P  O
O  L  R  R  R  B  J  F  G  M
L  E  I  O  A  T  S  O  O  B
L  A  V  F  R  C  D  E  I  I
E  S  E  N  V  I  S  I  O  N
V  E  N  E  R  G  I  Z  E  E
D  E  L  V  E  R  N  E  C  C
E  X  C  E  I  E  N  E  C  N
T  H  I  E  H  R  C  R  O  N
A  J  A  K  T  S  R  L  N  E
E  P  C  L  R  L  E  P  E  M
R  M  T  N  I  O  A  X  C  M
C  O  A  X  B  B  S  E  E  C
```

CREATE FIND-A-WORD

In the puzzle, find and circle the words listed below. Words can be found reading up, down, sideways, backward, and diagonally.

```
D   O   S   D   L   I   V   E
A   E   V   R   A   C   U   T
B   R   S   H   A   P   E   H
M   Q   P   I   O   N   M   C
C   A   B   E   G   I   N   N
D   E   K   F   G   N   L   U
B   A   K   E   H   I   J   A
L   R   U   F   N   U   K   L
```

BAKE   LAUNCH

BEGIN   MAKE

CARVE   SHAPE

DESIGN   UNFURL

CREATE FIND-A-WORD
ANSWER KEY

```
D   O   S   D   L   I   V   E
A   E   V   R   A   C   U   T
B   R   S   H   A   P   E   H
M   Q   P   I   O   N   M   C
C   A   B   E   G   I   N   N
D   E   K   F   G   N   L   U
B   A   K   E   H   I   J   A
L   R   U   F   N   U   K   L
```

GO FOR IT FIND-A-WORD

In the puzzle, find and circle the words listed below. Words can be found reading up, down, sideways, backward, and diagonally.

```
L  I  B  E  R  A  T  E  P  S
P  A  B  C  D  T  S  X  A  T
L  E  U  I  J  Z  A  P  R  R
O  F  G  N  K  A  L  E  T  E
W  O  H  E  C  L  B  R  I  N
E  R  T  G  L  H  M  I  C  G
Z  G  H  O  P  N  C  E  I  T
I  A  R  T  R  R  L  N  P  H
E  N  U  I  E  I  I  C  A  E
S  I  S  A  S  S  M  E  T  N
B  Z  T  T  S  K  B  P  E  L
A  E  L  E  C  R  O  F  E  E
R  P  R  O  P  E  L  A  Z  A
G  A  M  B  L  E  P  R  M  D
```

BLAST	GAMBLE	NEGOTIATE	RISK
CLIMB	GRAB	ORGANIZE	SEIZE
CREATE	LAUNCH	PARTICIPATE	STRENGTHEN
EXPERIENCE	LEAD	PLOW	THRUST
FORCE	LEAP	PRESS	
	LIBERATE	PROPEL	

GO FOR IT FIND-A-WORD
ANSWER KEY

L	I	B	E	R	A	T	E	P	S
P	A	B	C	D	T	S	X	A	T
L	E	U	I	J	Z	A	P	R	R
O	F	G	N	K	A	L	E	T	E
W	O	H	E	C	L	B	R	I	N
E	R	G	O	L	H	M	I	C	G
Z	G	T	T	P	N	C	E	I	T
I	A	R	I	R	R	L	N	P	H
E	N	U	A	E	I	I	C	A	E
S	I	S	S	S	S	M	E	T	N
B	Z	T	T	S	K	B	P	E	L
A	E	L	E	C	R	O	F	E	E
R	P	R	O	P	E	L	A	Z	A
G	A	M	B	L	E	P	R	M	D

ACTION BEGINS WITH 'E' FIND-A-WORD

In the puzzle, find and circle the words listed below. Words can be found reading up, down, sideways, backward, and diagonally.

```
E   M   B   A   R   K   O   E   P   R
N   M   V   Y   S   P   X   Q   O   E
L   E   A   W   T   T   N   U   L   S
I   L   X   N   R   I   M   I   E   C
G   E   C   A   C   H   C   P   T   A
H   C   C   B   R   I   E   D   C   P
T   T   G   A   T   F   P   C   H   E
E   M   E   R   G   E   B   A   Z   F
N   E   X   E   T   D   Z   I   T   E
E   N   P   E   I   Y   G   E   V   E
N   L   L   V   M   R   G   L   V   R
T   I   O   E   E   D   O   O   H   E
E   S   R   N   E   V   K   I   J   C
R   T   E   D   E   E   X   E   R   T
```

EDGE	EMERGE	ENTER	EVOKE
ELECT	EMIT	EQUIP	EVOLVE
ELICIT	ENERGIZE	ERECT	EXPLORE
EMANCIPATE	ENLIGHTEN	ESCAPE	EXTRACT
EMBARK	ENLIST	ETCH	

ACTION BEGINS WITH 'E'
FIND-A-WORD ANSWER KEY

E	M	B	A	R	K	O	E	P	R
N	M	V	Y	S	P	X	Q	O	E
L	E	A	W	T	T	N	U	L	S
I	L	X	N	R	I	M	I	E	C
G	E	C	A	C	H	C	P	T	A
H	C	C	B	R	I	E	D	C	P
T	T	G	A	T	F	P	C	H	E
E	M	E	R	G	E	B	A	Z	F
N	E	X	E	T	D	Z	I	T	E
E	N	P	E	I	Y	G	F	V	F
N	L	L	V	M	R	G	L	V	R
T	I	O	E	E	D	O	O	H	E
E	S	R	N	F	V	K	I	J	C
R	T	E	D	E	X	E	R	R	T

WORZLES (WORD PUZZLES)

Purpose

To raise awareness of the inevitability of change.

Play Time

10 minutes

Physical Activity

None

Participation Format

Individual

Materials and Preparation

Copy of Worzle sheet for each participant

Pencils

Flip chart displaying Worzle Answer Key

Directions

1. Before a break, announce that a Worzle (Word Puzzle) will be placed at each person's seat and that participants may start the game as soon as the break is over. Tell participants that those who are punctual will have a competitive advantage.

2. Distribute sheets near the end of the break.

3. When the break is over, instruct the participants to complete the Worzle. Announce that 1 or more winners will be determined, based on the highest number of correct answers completed within 5 minutes.

4. Let participants know when their playing time has elapsed.

5. Review answers with the group by asking for volunteers to provide them. Refer to the flip chart. Ask each person to keep track of his or her correct answers.

6. Identify and acknowledge those with the highest number of correct answers. Award prizes if you choose.

Debriefing

Discuss with participants their reactions to the words in the exercise and their insights about change.

ORGANIZATIONAL CHANGE WORZLES (WORD PUZZLES)

Decipher the following Worzles that are related to organizational change:

1. Change Change Change Change Change Chang e Change Change Chan ge Change Change Cha	**2.** times times **times** t i m e s t i m e s times **times** *times* TIMES t i m e s t i m e s
3. Budget	**4.** Money Money Money
5. S I Z I N G	**6.** Budget ————————— Coming In
7. Com mitments	**8.** ————————— ————————— ————————— Results

ORGANIZATIONAL CHANGE WORZLES (WORD PUZZLES) ANSWER KEY

1. Constant or continual change
2. Changing times
3. Budget on target
4. No money left
5. Downsizing
6. Coming in under budget
7. Broken commitments
8. Bottom-line results

THINGS THAT CHANGE
WORZLES (WORD PUZZLES)

Decipher the following Worzles that are related to things that change:

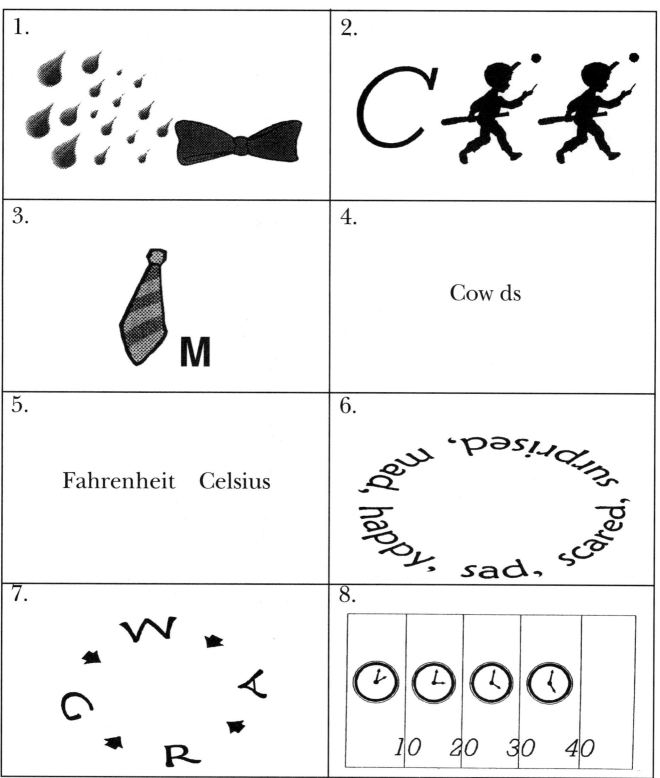

THINGS THAT CHANGE WORZLES (WORD PUZZLES) ANSWER KEY

1. Rainbows
2. Seasons
3. Time
4. Moods
5. Temperature
6. Mood ring
7. Hologram
8. Time zones

Bibliography

Beckhard, Richard, and Reuben T. Harris. *Organizational Transitions: Managing Complex Change.* Reading, MA: Addison-Wesley Publishing Company, 1987.

Beckhard, Richard, and Wendy Pritchard. *Changing the Essence: The Art of Creating and Leading Fundamental Change in Organizations.* San Francisco: Jossey-Bass Publishers, 1992.

Bridges, William. *Managing Transitions: Making the Most of Change.* Reading, MA: Perseus Books, 1991.

Bridges, William. *Transitions: Making Sense of Life's Changes.* Reading, MA: Addison-Wesley Publishing Company, 1980.

Brock, Lillie R., and Mary Ann Salerno. *The InterChange Cycle™: Managing Life Means Managing the Changes.* Falls Church, VA: Bridge Builder Media, 1994.

Conner, Daryl R. *Managing at the Speed of Change.* New York: Villard Books (a division of Random House), 1992.

Dalziel, Murray M., and Stephen C. Schoonover. *Changing Ways: A Practical Tool for Implementing Change within Organizations.* New York: AMACOM, 1988.

Herrmann, Ned. *The Whole Brain Business Book: Unlocking the Power of Whole Brain Thinking in Organizations and Individuals.* New York: McGraw-Hill, 1996.

Kanter, Rosabeth Moss, Barry A. Stein, and Todd D. Jick. *The Challenge of Organizational Change: How Companies Experience It and Leaders Guide It.* New York: The Free Press (a division of Macmillan, Inc.), 1992.

Katzenbach, Jon R., and the RCL Team. *Real Change Leaders: How You Can Create Growth and High Performance at Your Company.* New York: Times Business (a division of Random House), 1995.

Kotter, John P. *Leading Change.* Boston: Harvard Business School Press, 1996.

Kouzes, James M., and Barry Z. Posner. *The Leadership Challenge: How to Get Extraordinary Things Done in Organizations.* San Francisco: Jossey-Bass Publishers, 1987.

Mauer, Rick. *Beyond the Wall of Resistance.* Austin, TX: Bard Books, Inc., 1996.

Nadler, David A. Robert B. Shaw, and A. Elise Walton and Associates. *Discontinuous Change.* San Francisco: Jossey-Bass Publishers, 1995.

Nanus, Burt. *Visionary Leadership.* San Francisco: Jossey-Bass Publishers, 1992.

Olesen, Erik. *Mastering the Winds of Change: Peak Performers Reveal How to Stay on Top in Times of Turmoil.* New York: HarperBusiness (division of HarperCollinsPublishers), 1994.

Peters, Tom. *The Pursuit of WOW! Every Person's Guide to Topsy-Turvy Times.* New York: Vintage Books (a division of Random House, Inc.), 1993.

Potter, Beverly. *The Way of the Ronin: Riding the Waves of Change at Work.* Berkeley, CA: Ronin Publishing, Inc., 1984.

Scott, Cynthia D., and Dennis T. Jaffe. *Managing Change at Work.* Menlo Park, CA: Crisp Publications, Inc., 1995.

Siebert, Al. *The Survivor Personality.* Portland, OR: Practical Psychology Press, 1994.

Smith, Douglas K. *Taking Charge of Change: 10 Principles for Managing People and Performance.* Reading, MA: Addison-Wesley Publishing Company, 1996.

Sujansky, Joanne G. *The Power of Partnering: Vision, Commitment, and Action.* San Diego, CA: Pfeiffer & Company, 1991.

Yukl, Gary. Leadership in Organizations. Upper Saddle River, NJ: Prentice Hall, 1981 (and 1989, 1994, and 1998).

About the Authors

Dr. Suzanne A. Schmidt co-owns and manages Renewal Resources, a consulting practice that specializes in change management, leadership, organizational renewal, and team-building. She teaches in the University of Maryland Graduate School and has extensive experience managing human resources for Fortune 500 companies.

Dr. Joanne G. Sujansky owns and manages Training Connection, an 18-year-old management consulting and training firm that specializes in change management. She was the national president of the American Society for Training & Development in 1985 and has worked in 25 countries as a speaker, trainer, and consultant. A Certified Speaking Professional, Dr. Sujansky gives over 100 speeches and training presentations a year, reaching more than 10,000 people. She is the author of two books, *The Power of Partnering* (Pfeiffer, 1990) and *Putting Change in Your Pocket* (Training Connection, 1996).